# HOMOPHONES:
## Sonic Wonders

## H ä m- ə - fōn
Hom = Same     Phone = Sound

Joyce Reinholds

WESTBOW
P R E S S®
A DIVISION OF THOMAS NELSON
& ZONDERVAN

WestBow Press books may be ordered through booksellers or by contacting:

WestBow Press
A Division of Thomas Nelson & Zondervan
1663 Liberty Drive
Bloomington, IN 47403
www.westbowpress.com
1 (866) 928-1240

ISBN: 978-1-9736-0234-7 (sc)
ISBN: 978-1-9736-0235-4 (e)

Library of Congress Control Number: 2017914605

Print information available on the last page.

WestBow Press rev. date: 2/2/2018

To my inspiration, Priel and Natania, two of my granddaughters.

To my parents, for the rich heritage they gave me.

To my husband, who suggested many of the sets of words and encouraged me in so many ways.

To the many friends who encouraged me, gave many suggestions, and prayed for me.

# PREFACE

For Christmas 1964, my mother and dad gave me a *Webster's Seventh New Collegiate Dictionary* published by G. & C. Merriam Company in 1963. In the front was glued a typed note that said:

> This book is intended to be your most valuable possession; treasure it and use it daily. Whenever you read another book, keep this one within arm's reach and use it to look up every word that you do not understand.

> Abraham Lincoln said, "I will study and get ready—and some day my chance may come."

Many times I have seen my dad, who passed away in 1992 at age eighty-five, reading a book with his dictionary within arm's reach. He was a man who always inspired me to study, though his own opportunities were limited in his youth. He was compelled to drop out of school in the eighth grade in order to work to support his widowed mother and siblings. He finally earned his high school diploma in 1962, the same year my older sister graduated from high school.

After his death, I found many certificates of completion from various correspondence schools, so though his opportunities for formal education were few in his youth, he had the self-discipline to do what he could.

His propensity for study proved itself during World War II, when he attained the rank of chief in eighteen months, which was the fastest time his superior could legally manage.

After World War II my dad worked for the US Navy as a civil servant on Treasure Island until his retirement in 1969. While there, the navy offered many classes to the employees, among them English classes. My dad used to drill me on the lessons he learned in that course. Though I do not remember the course's name, I do remember that it was nothing like what I was being taught in school, and the lessons presented were very practical.

So I have my dad to thank for instilling in me a love of learning. He also instilled in me the determination to finish a project well. Thus it is with this book. What began as a clever idea morphed into a work that cannot help but divulge much of my philosophy of life while simultaneously attempting to dissect the English language. May I help you a bit in your journey of life as well as in your understanding of the English language?

Have fun as you study! Like Abraham Lincoln, some day your chance may come.

# INTRODUCTION

Homonyms are two or more words that sound alike and look alike but don't mean the same thing. Homophones sound the same but are spelled differently and, of course, mean very different things. It is the homophone that we will address in this book.

My mother, who was born in 1905, told me that when she was in school, she learned to spell words with guidance from dictionary pronunciation symbols. The upside-down e (ə) was her favorite. She said the pronunciation symbols did not confuse her when it came to spelling the words correctly. I was not raised on such a system but became motivated when my granddaughter, Priel (Prē-əl), was learning to read. I began to make a list of words that sound the same but are spelled differently and have *very* different meanings. How confusing such words must be to a child and to those learning English as a foreign language!

One problem is that even two Webster's dictionaries have different pronunciation keys, so I have chosen symbols found in *Webster's Encyclopedic Unabridged Dictionary of the English Language* published in 1989 by Portland House, New York, since I was able to download the symbols listed in that dictionary from the wikipedia website.[1]

The pronunciation key is located at the beginning of this book and contains only the vowel sounds used in this book.

The 197 sets of words contained in this book are by no means an exhaustive list; you will think of other sets, I am sure. I did not consult any other source when choosing the words; they came up in daily conversations or signs along the road. I didn't even think to consult the Internet! Two sets of words should have been included in this book, (f(ə)r) and (nō). *Fir* is a type of tree and *fur* is the hair of

---

[1] accessed August 21, 2017 http://en.wikipedia.org/wiki/Pronunciation_respelling_for_English

an animal. *Know* means to understand and *no* means negative. How many more homophone sets can you discover? Even (fōr-wƏrd), as in "Forward, march!" or its sound-alike, the foreword to this book, are good pairs!

*Homophones: Sonic Wonders* is a workbook designed for learners in grades three to eight but is also very suitable for those wishing to brush up on basic English skills that they may have missed in school. It is also very appropriate for English as a second language learners who also want to learn about American cultural literacy.

Hopefully, from the context of the sentences the reader will figure out the meaning of unfamiliar words. If not, readers should look the words up in the dictionary. The words are presented in order of difficulty, and each level has a word search and a crossword puzzle to give readers more practice.[2] The answers to the fill-in sentences are listed in alphabetical order in the back of the book. Depending on their educational goals, readers may just skip to the back and read those sentences. Do the puzzles or not. The table of contents lists all words for each of the ten levels presented. The index in the back lists all words in alphabetical order and the level in which they can be found. Let your own abilities and needs dictate how you study the book. The English language is full of enigmas. May this workbook help you to solve many of them.

---

[2] All puzzles in this book created at www.puzzle-maker.com.

# PRONUNCIATION KEY

ā aid, cape, way

â â(r) (a (ə) r) air, dare, Mary

ä alms, art, calm

ch chief, butcher, beach

ə occurs only in unaccented syllables and indicates the sound of

> *a* in alone
>
> *e* in system
>
> *i* in easily
>
> *o* in gallop
>
> *u* in circus

small ə occurs in unaccented syllables before l preceded by *t, d,* or *n*

or before *n* preceded by *t* or *d* to show syllabic quality as in:

> cradle
>
> redden
>
> metal
>
> mental
>
> and in accented syllables between long *i* and *r*
>
> to show diphthongal quality, as in fire and hire

ē equal, seat, bee, mighty

ēr ear, mere

ī ice, bite, pirate, deny

ng sing, Washington

ô ought, ball, raw

ō over, boat, know

o͝o book

o͞o ooze, fool, too

ou out, loud, prow

ow out, loud, prow

# LEVEL 1

Please write (rīt) the correct answers in the spaces provided.

**Ate Eight 8 VIII** (āt)
I _____(āt) _____(āt) cookies and came down with a
very bad tummy ache!
Do you know how many _____ (āt) is? Too many, that's for sure!
I will never eat _____ (āt) cookies at once again!
The Arabic numeral for the number eight is _____.
King Henry _____ started the Church of England.

**Be Bee** (bē)
Pretty buzzing bumble_____ (bē),
Won't you please _____ (bē) nice to me?
Please don't sting me!
"To _____ (bē) or not to _____ (bē),
That is the question."[3]
Do you want to _____ (bē) a _____ (bē) when you grow up?

**Blew Blue** (blo͞o)
The wind _____ (blo͞o) away the clouds, so now I can see the
_____(blo͞o) sky.

**Knows Nose** (nōz)
Priel _____ (nōz) that her _____ (nōz) helps her smell.
She _____ (nōz) sometimes the smell is pleasant, and sometimes
her _____ (nōz) tells her something *stinks!*

---
[3] Shakespeare, William, *The Tragedy of Hamlet, Prince of Denmark,* Act III Scene 1.

**One Won** (w(ə)n)

Kristy is the _____ (w(ə)n) who _____ (w(ə)n) the Princess Race at Disneyland.

**Read Red** (red)

I _____ (red) the story of Little _____ (red) Riding Hood and liked it very much until I _____ (red) about the wolf trying to trick the girl and put her in danger.[4]

**Sea See** (sē)

I want to _____ (sē) the ocean and _____ (sē) for myself the majesty of the waves of the _____crashing on the shore.

[4] Arthur Rackham, The *Arthur Fairy Book* (Philadelphia: J.B. Lippincott Company, 1930), 266–268. http://www.eastoftheweb.com/short-stories/UBooks/LittRed.shtml.

In a Word Search, a word may appear normal or backwards,

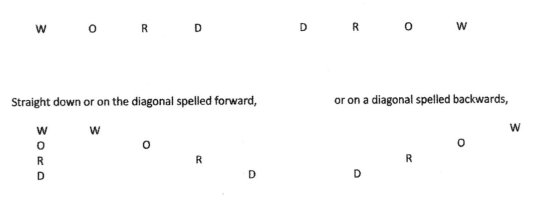

W      O      R      D           D      R      O      W

Straight down or on the diagonal spelled forward,        or on a diagonal spelled backwards,

```
W    W                                                        W
O         O                                            O
R              R                                  R
D                   D                   D
```

Straight down spelled backwards, on a diagonal spelled backwards, or on a diagonal spelled normally.

```
D    D                                                        D
R         R                                         R
O              O                        O
W                   W         W
```

In a Crossword Puzzle, there are only two possibilities of word order: across or down. The number in the box corresponds to the clue at the bottom of the page. Here is an example where the W shares a box across and down and in this case, the answer is the same for across and down:

| 1 W | O | R | D |
|---|---|---|---|
| O | | | |
| R | | | |
| D | | | |

Across

1 A sentence has at least one _____ .

Down

1 "Let me give you a _____ of wisdom."

3

# Level 1 Crossword

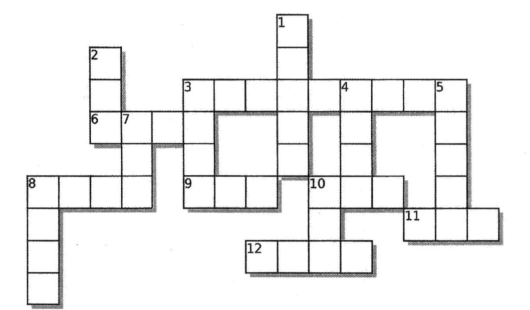

ACROSS

3  Words sound same, meaning differs
6  I smell with my _____
8  The color the sky usually is
9  Little _____ Riding Hood
10 I _____ with my eyes
11 Past tense of eat
12 I _____ the story out loud

DOWN

1  Tommy _____ better
2  They lost and we _____
3  My ears help me _____
4  Please come _____
5  I am 8 years old
7  I have two ears but _____ mouth
8  What the wind did
10 There are many fish in the _____

4

# Level 1 Word Search

```
H O M O P H O N E E
W E L B T S E A G
O B U H S W O N K
N A G L R E D R G
E I T A B E E B D
E S E E R A E O R
E H O E D E N T R
S M H N D E B R T
```

| | |
|---|---|
| Homophone | Here |
| Ate | Knows |
| Eight | Nose |
| Be | One |
| Bee | Read |
| Blew | Red |
| Blue | Sea |
| Hear | See |
| | Won |

5

# LEVEL 2

Please write (rīt) the correct answers in the spaces provided.

**Bare Bear** (ba(ə)r)
My favorite toy as a child was a teddy _____ (ba(ə)r) that was pink and had polka dots on its tummy.
The _____ (ba(ə)r)—not my teddy _____ (ba(ə)r))—stripped the tree _____ (ba(ə)r) of its bark.
Lydia is my best friend. With her I can _____ (ba(ə)r) my soul and tell her my most private secrets.

**By buy bye** (bī)
I will _____ (bī) some flowers to give to my friend when I have to say _____ (bī).
"_____ (bī)" is a quick remark at the end of a phone conversation.
Please pick me some flowers _____ (bī) 2 p.m.

**In Inn** (in)
I was disappointed when my husband told me there was no vacant room _____ (in) the _____ (in) for us to stay.

**Knew New** (no͞o)
Tina ran outside in the rain in her _____ (no͞o) shoes even though she _____ (no͞o) better. Tina's brother _____ (no͞o) their mother would be angry!

6

**Lo Low** (lō)

And, _____ (lō), the angel of the Lord appeared.[5]
The animals _____(lō) in the stable, giving thanks for the savior in their own special way.

**Pail Pale** (pā(ə)l)

Jack and Jill went up the hill to fetch a _____ (pā(ə)l) of water.
Jill became _____ (pā(ə)l) when Jack fell down and spilled his _____ (pā(ə)l) of water!

**Shoe Shoo** (sho͞o)

_____ (sho͞o), fly, don't bother me
For I belong to somebody!
I must _____ (sho͞o) away that fly because I certainly will never be able to get him with my _____ (sho͞o).

**Son Sun** (s(ə)n)

If my _____(s(ə)n) spends a lot of time in the _____(s(ə)n), he will get a _____(s(ə)n)burn.

**Toe Tow** (tō)

It would be a very silly thing to see a tugboat _____(tō) my _____ (tō)! But maybe I can imagine that a tugboat will _____(tō) my _____ (tō) when I don't want to get out of bed in the morning.

---

[5] Luke 2:9, King James Version

# Level 2 Crossword

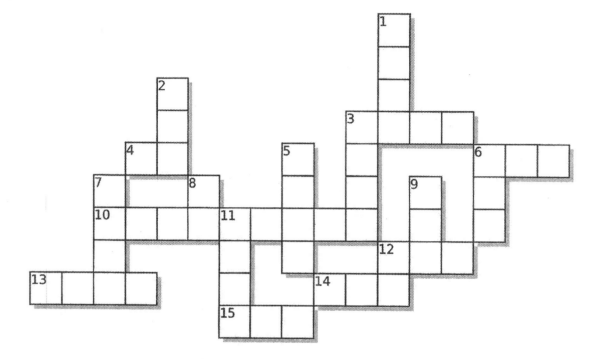

ACROSS

3   A big, furry animal
4   Beside
6   If the car breaks down
    we will need a _____
    truck
10  Words sound same,
    meaning differs
12  A type of hotel
13  Tommy _____ the
    answer
14  I have one daughter
    and one _____
15  We singers have a high
    voice and a _____ voice

DOWN

1   When sick I look _____
2   Purchase
3   No covering
5   _____ that fly away
    from me
6   I have this on the end
    of my foot
7   John lost two socks and
    one _____
8   A shout of surprise
9   Rain and the _____
    helps plants grow
11  A _____ is a bucket
12  Inside

# Level 2 Word Search

```
H Q L M N N Y N P Y M D P
O D T Y T G W Q A I N A E
M X M T Y E N Q I Y L O M
O N P D N J R J L E H Y N
P L N K Q A N L W S W O L
H T T I E M Y E T O S L O
O E K B S M L O W N T Z T
N D R Y B H E N W R W Y L
E B D A B U O D R S B N T
K Y G N B Q Y O U N D Q N
N E Y K R B J N Q N D Y G
W B V G N B M Z V R T J P
```

| | |
|---|---|
| Homophone | Lo |
| Bare | Low |
| Bear | Pail |
| By | Pale |
| Buy | Shoe |
| Bye | Shoo |
| In | Son |
| Inn | Sun |
| Knew | Toe |
| New | Tow |

# LEVEL 3

Please write (rīt) the correct answers in the spaces provided.

**Beat Beet** (bēt)
The recipe says to _____ (bēt) the cake batter for two minutes.
I am going to _____ (bēt) you in a race. I will eat every _____
(bēt) on my plate before you eat all of yours! (That makes Mother
mad. It is bad manners to gulp down my food.)

**Cell Sell** (sel)
If you _____ (sel) things that are not legal to _____ (sel),
you may end up in a jail _____ (sel).
The building block of the human body is the _____ (sel).
The phone company tried to _____ (sel) me a _____ (sel)
phone.

**Dear Deer** (di(ə)r)
The story of Bambi, the little _____ (di(ə)r), is _____ (di(ə)r)
to my heart.

**Fair Fare** (fa(ə)r)
What is the _____ (fa(ə)r) to enter the _____ (fa(ə)r)?

**Flour Flower** (flow(ə)r)
When I was young, I used to play with white _____ (flow(ə)r)
and pretend it was snow.
The crocus is often the first _____ (flow(ə)r) to push its way
through the snow in the spring.

**Heal Heel** (hē(ə)l)
I just bought some shoes that support my feet better. Now perhaps my _____ (hē(ə)l) will have a chance to _____ (hē(ə)l) so it will no longer be painful when I walk.


**Main Mane** (mān)
Simba thought he would be the _____ (mān) event when he was big enough to have a _____ (mān) and a roar!


**Meat Meet** (mēt)
I would like to _____ (mēt) somebody who prefers _____ (mēt) to tofu for dinner!


**Peak Peek** (pēk)
That mountain _____(pēk) is beautiful in the sunset.
At Christmastime, every child will _____(pēk) at the presents under the tree!


**Ray RE** (rā)
_____(rā) is the second tone of the diatonic scale. (See DO.)
It is beautiful to be in a forest and trace a _____(rā) of sunshine as it travels through the tree limbs to the path below.
The _____(rā) belongs to an order of fish that has a flat body and eyes on its top side. When snorkeling, it is hard to see the _____(rā) as it rests on the sandy ocean bottom, especially when only occasionally is there a _____(rā) of sunshine that reaches the ocean floor. I wonder if the _____(rā) can sing, "_____(rā)"?

**Right Write Rite Wright** (rīt)

Most people know the difference between _____ (rīt) and wrong.

Did you know that a _____ (rīt) is a workman of wood?

With which hand do you _____ (rīt)? The left or the _____ (rīt)?

We must always strive to do the _____ (rīt) thing. A religious _____ (rīt) can help us focus on God in worship so we can ask him to help us do the _____ (rīt) thing in every situation.

**Scene Seen** (sēn)

I have never _____ (sēn) such a beautiful _____ (sēn) in all my life!

**Tea Tee TI** (tē)

_____ (tē) is the seventh note of diatonic scale, sometimes called si. (See DO.)

I like a nice cup of hot _____ (tē) when I am cold.

Place your golf ball very carefully on the _____ (tē) so you can start your game with confidence!

When writing a story, sometimes an author will have a character laugh by saying, "_____ (tē)-hee!"

# Level 3 Crossword

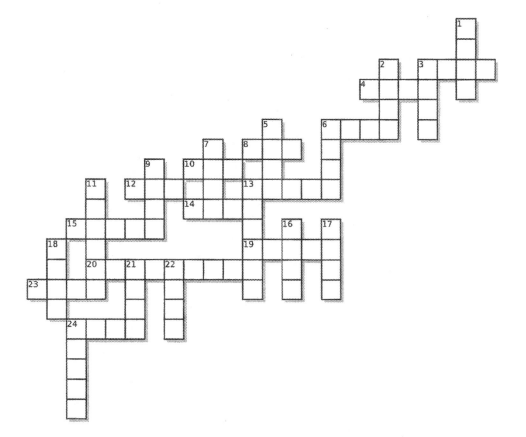

ACROSS

3   Will I be able to _____ your family?
4   The shaggy hair around a lion's face
6   Bambi
8   In order to play golf, you need a ____
10  Hope is like a _____ of sunshine
12  Please have a cup of ____ with me.
13  What is needed to make cookies or bread
14  Building block of the human body
15  Always do the _____ thing
19  _____ your name on your paper
20  Words sound same, meaning differs
23  A vegtable
24  Have you _____ my friend?

DOWN

1   Did you _____ at the presents?
2   Do you like the rides at the _____
3   A carnivore eats _____
5   To offer for a price
6   Precious
7   The fee
9   To win a race
11  A _____ is a worker in wood
13  Give to someone you love
16  Communion is a religious _____
17  To recover from being hurt
18  The first part of your foot to touch the
    ground when you walk
21  Primary
22  I'd like to visit Pikes _____
24  A lake surrounded by trees is a beautiful

    _____

13

# Level 3 Word Search

```
H Z E T F E H P E A K K R
O V N H L R N E R I T E J
M P A G O X I E A S E E N
O R M I U H T G C L V X B
P T E R R A E D H S M F D
H P W W E Y E E C T A B L
O K F B O A V E L I E M G
N M R A R L L T R E A L Q
E E E E R L F I T I L K D
W E T A E E N R N E E T L
R T E E T D L W S E Y A R
R M L T A T Y B P V K Y M
```

Homophone
Beat
Beet
Cell
Sell
Dear
Deer
Fair
Fare
Flour
Flower
Heal
Heel
Main

Mane
Meat
Meet
Peak
Peek
Ray
Right
Rite
Scene
Seen
Tea
Tee
Write
Wright

# LEVEL 4

Please write (rīt) the correct answers in the spaces provided.

**Beau Bow** (bō)
When I was a little girl, my dad was always the best at tying the
_____ (bō) at the back of my dress. Do you think that a _____
(bō) at the back of a dress was still in style when I was old enough
to have a _____ (bō)?
The string on a _____ (bō) must be pulled taut in order to shoot
the arrow far enough to reach its target.
One must have a good quality _____ (bō) to make a cello or
violin sound lovely.

**Chews Choose** (ch(o͞o)z)
Priel _____ (ch(o͞o)z) the stick of gum until there is no taste left
in it. She then will have to _____ (ch(o͞o)z) a new piece of gum
if she wants it to have a good taste.

**Ewe You** (yo͞o)
Cindy, _____ (yo͞o) were so cute in the Christmas program,
playing the _____ (yo͞o) resting with her baby lamb near the
manger.

**Flea Flee** (flē)
That pesky _____ (flē) had better _____ (flē) from me!

**Hair Hare** (ha(ə)r)
I must be getting healthier. My _____ (ha(ə)r) is turning back
to gray after having been white for many years! It must be the trace

15

minerals in the blackstrap molasses I have been eating for several months.

A _____ (ha(ə)r) is very much like a rabbit.

The _____ (ha(ə)r) of a _____ (ha(ə)r) is called fur.

## Hour Our ((ou)(ə)r)

The soup kitchen has asked us to spend just one _____ ((ou)(ə)r) of _____ ((ou)(ə)r) time serving food to the homeless so the needy people can have a chance to eat.

## Me MI (mē)

_____ (mē) is the third tone of the diatonic scale. _____(mē) is a name I call myself, according to the "DO, a Deer" song.[6]

Will you sing for _____ (mē)?

## None Nun (n(ə)n)

There were _____ (n(ə)n) who would volunteer to work at the leper colony except one _____ (n(ə)n) who was willing to risk her life to help the needy. There were _____ (n(ə)n) so brave as she! _____ (n(ə)n) dare try to talk the _____ (n(ə)n) out of her devotion!

## Plain Plane (plān)

In the United States, the middle of the country is one vast _____ (plān).

A carpenter uses a _____ (plān) to make a wood surface level and smooth.

We go to an airport to catch an airplane but we call it a _____ (plān).

It is _____ (plān) to see that an airstrip is easier to create on the _____ (plān) than in the mountains.

A _____ (plān) can only land on a _____ (plān) surface.

---

[6] 6 Richard Rodgers and Oscar Hammerstein II, "DO, a Deer," *The Sound of Music* New York: Williamson Music, INC., 1959, 16-21

**Read Reed** (rēd)

Please _____ (rēd) me the story of a little girl getting lost in the _____ (rēd) swamp.

**Role Roll** (rōl)

In a family, hopefully there is one member who plays the _____ (rōl) of peacemaker.

Gretchen danced the _____ (rōl) of Giselle in the ballet, *Giselle.*

At Christmastime it is fun to _____ (rōl) out cookie dough and use a cookie cutter to make a gingerbread man.

At a restaurant, we like to ask for a _____ (rōl) instead of the cheese bread they usually offer.

Priel and Natania will _____ (rōl) down the hill at the park, giggling all the time.

**Tail Tale** (tā(ə)l)

An elephant has a funny _____ (tā(ə)l),

A fox, a bushy one.

But Paul Bunyan could spin a tall _____ (tā(ə)l).

In fact, he *became* one! (Note: "spin" means to tell.)

**Weak Week** (wēk)

I have had the flu and have felt _____ (wēk) all _____ (wēk).

# Level 4 Crossword

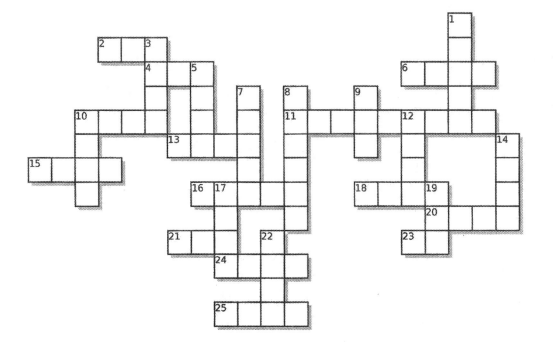

ACROSS

2  A woman who becomes part of
   a religious order
4  This is ____ house
6  A serious boyfriend or girlfriend
10 What ____ do you play in the
   production?
11 Words sound same, meaning
   differs
13 An insect
15 To run away quickly
16 To chomp with the teeth
18 A kind of wild rabbit
20 Not strong
21 I am I and ____ are ____
23 Please give ___ a chance
24 Did you _____ a story to Sarah?
25 A _____ is an old, old story.

DOWN

1  Judy is fancy but I am
3  Mother Hubbard's doggie had
   ____
5  You can eat a _____ or you
   can _____ down a hill
7  We will catch a _____ at the
   airport
8  To select
9  A pretty decoration
10 A _____ is a plant.
12 Brush your _____ 100
   strokes every day
14 Seven days
17 I only want one _____ of your
   time
19 A mama sheep
22 A dog will wag his _____ if
   he likes you.

# Level 4 Word Search

```
E M G D J D B N J X R G L K V M
S P N N T A M E E K T L T D W J
O P U P T E B N T A L E P E N N
O N W N J R O P G M N R R T T T
H M Y N B H B R L K L A E C N Q
C Q N H P F L E A A H F H E W E
W O B O L K R E U T I E L N D V
P P M U N E W U J O W N X E Y T
J O L R Z E R Y O S Y M D M E V
H D R A Q W R O Y R Y W T B B N
K B R Q N J I Y L L J M L E D Y
P L K L J E A Y L E B I A R P R
L D Y J D M H V T L A U L X Z M
T M D M B R N G J T O M T B M D
R L W B R Q K M K D P R Q D Q K
```

| | |
|---|---|
| Homophone | Nun |
| Beau | Our |
| Bow | Plain |
| Chews | Plane |
| Choose | Read |
| Ewe | Reed |
| Flea | Role |
| Flee | Roll |
| Hair | Tail |
| Hare | Tale |
| Hour | Weak |
| Me | Week |
| None | You |

# LEVEL 5

Please write (rīt) the correct answers in the spaces provided.

**Aye I Eye** (ī)

_____ (ī)-, _____ (ī), Captain! _____ (ī) can see that ship through the (ī)_____glass (one word).

**Board Bored** (bō(ə)rd)

When I was bad in school I had to write on the _____ (bō(ə)rd), "I will behave in school," so many times that I became _____ (bō(ə)rd).

**Creak Creek** (krēk)

The sound of the _____ (krēk) flowing by the house can mask the sound of the _____ (krēk) in the board on the stair when I am trying to sneak back into my room late at night.

**Days Daze** (dāz)

After so many _____ (dāz) of travel on our trip, we were in a _____ (dāz) when we finally arrived at our destination.

**DO Doe Dough** (dō)

_____ (dō) is the first syllable of the diatonic scale in solmization. (The entire scale is <u>DO</u> RE MI FA SOL LA TI <u>DO</u>.)"_____(dō), a deer, a female deer," are the first few words of the "_____(dō), a Deer" song from the *Sound Of Music*.[7] The female deer is really a _____ (dō).

My sister used to eat biscuit _____ (dō) when she was young. *Ugh!* I much preferred oatmeal cookie _____ (dō).

---

[7] Richard Rodgers and Oscar Hammerstein II, "DO, a Deer," *The Sound of Music* New York: Williamson Music, INC., 1959, 16-21

**Grease Greece** (grēs)

The smell of bacon _____ (grēs) is a pleasant smell, especially when cooking over a campfire.

Do they cook like that in the nation of _____ (grēs)?

**Heard Herd** (h(ə)rd)

The _____ (h(ə)rd) of cattle started to stampede when they _____ (h(ə)rd) the shot of a rifle.

**Him Hymn** (him)

A favorite _____ (him) of many people is "In the Garden."

God loves to hear a _____ (him) of praise sung to honor _____ (him).

**Hole Whole** (hōl)

If I have a _____ (hōl) in my purse, my _____ (hōl) collection of coins could be lost.

**Mail Male** (mā(ə)l)

A little boy is a _____ (mā(ə)l) who will grow up to be a daddy.

Maybe he will work for the post office and deliver _____ (mā(ə)l) for a living.

**Might Mite** mīt)

I _____ (mīt) get very annoyed by a _____ (mīt) if it chooses to bite me!

**Night Knight** (nīt)

The medieval _____ (nīt) was a warrior who wanted to be seen.

He had no desire to fight at _____ (nīt) when it was dark.

**Passed Past** (past)

In the _____(past), Cheryl always studied and _____(past) all her exams easily, so why is she nervous now?

**Peace Piece** (pēs)

What _____ (pēs) I have, floating on this lake in my boat.
Wouldn't everyone like to have a _____ (pēs) of my happiness?


**Rose Rows** (rōz)

At the park there were _____ (rōz) and _____ (rōz) of
_____ (rōz) bushes of every imaginable color a _____
(rōz) could be.
In *Romeo and Juliet*, Shakespeare wrote, "A _____ (rōz) by
any other name would smell as sweet," but I think a _____ (rōz)
called a stink bud would *not* smell so pretty.


**Sail Sale** (sā(ə)l)

I made a _____ (sā(ə)l) out of fabric I purchased on _____
(sā(ə)l) at the fabric store. My boat should _____ (sā(ə)l) far with
such a _____ (sā(ə)l)! Maybe I can purchase some boat paint
on _____ (sā(ə)l) too at the paint store.


**Sew So SO Sow** (sō)

_____ (sō) is the fifth degree of the diatonic scale. (See DO.)
I am _____ (sō) weary after making a quilt for a great-grandson but
was _____ (sō) energized by the gratitude of my granddaughter.
I will _____ (sō) again soon!
We think to _____ (sō) seed by hand is rather old-fashioned,
but I still like to spread lawn fertilizer that way.


**Shirley Surely** (shû(r)-lē)

_____ (shû(r)-lē) you have heard of _____ (shû(r)-lē)
Temple, the cute dimpled film star who cheered audiences during
the Depression.

**Their There They're** (thər)

I thought it was here that I left my book, but I see it over _____ (thər) by the clock. Did you notice that the word *here* is contained in the word _____ (thər)? That is a good memory tip: here and _____ (thər) are both places, one close and one far.

The sports fans had _____ (thər) eyes on the star player. _____ (thər) hoping he will save the game!

_____ (thər) means "they are." An apostrophe is in place of the letter *a* to make a contraction.

_____ (thər) afraid of _____ (thər) own shadow over _____ (thər) on that dark street.

# Level 5 Crossword

ACROSS

2  In order to
3  Carpenters use
6  Tiny bug
7  Opposite of future
10 Stunned
12 Letters received
14 A sound in a haunted house
16 Done with needle and thread
17 A man
18 My bag has a _____ in it
19 To her or to ____
20 Maybe
24 Words sound same, meaning differs
25 Scatter seed
28 Tranquil
29 A country
31 Seven ____ in a week
33 My ___ helps me see
34 Nothing to do
35 A sailor's way to say yes

DOWN

1  An arrangement of chairs
2  A boat is moved by the wind
4  Unbaked bread or cookies
5  A group of animals
7  A part of
8  The stars are seen at _____
9  Flower
11 Listened
13 Me, myself, and ___
15 A soldier of feudal days
19 A song of praise
21 Used to fry foods
22 _____ Temple
23 Entire
26 Certainly
27 A small river
30 To hand to another
31 Female Deer
32 Available for purchase

# Level 5 Word Search

```
G T T N P Y G Q T M E W P N T N H I M
L R H D M Q P N B R S Y E N J C L N J
P I E G D E R O B M H B A S R P Q X B
K A A A I D O U G H I E C E E R G T T
Z O S S S N K J N B R T E X N P H Q J
S R L S L E K T G Y L K E L D G T S N
K M G I E D L B W N E D I E I A A D M
Z A A P O D N M Y H Y P L N L L Y T T
B M E E Z R H D L E P I E C E A S S T
Y L E R U S E K X L N H O L E A M V Y
T W X M C R A L J Y Q O M Q P Y R W V
Y D N K O R R D N R Y W H O L E N D V
T R B S O P D N Q R D J M P J G V G R
B E E W Q W E D E G W I W L O T P R D
O H S M J M M A Z Z G N P T Q M D Q V
A Q X X Y M D P C H A E Y E K B O M R
R Z T V T K P Y T E L D W O S W Y H R
D Y R Z J R R J R D N N D L Y V P V R
```

| | |
|---|---|
| Homophone | Knight |
| Aye | Mail |
| Eye | Male |
| Board | Might |
| Bored | Mite |
| Creak | Night |
| Creek | Passed |
| Days | Past |
| Daze | Peace |
| Doe | Piece |
| Dough | Rose |
| Grease | Rows |
| Greece | Sail |
| Heard | Sale |
| Herd | Sew |
| Him | Shirley |
| Hole | So |
| Hymn | Sow |
| I | Surely |
| | Whole |

# LEVEL 6

Please write (rīt) the correct answers in the spaces provided.

**Aid Aide** (ād)
A person who will _____ (ād) another is a special helper called an _____ (ād).

**Aisle Isle I'll** (īl)
An _____(īl) is straight, but an _____(īl) is round.
_____(īl) help set up the chairs in the auditorium so that an_____(īl) is created for easy access for the patrons.

**Billed Build** (bild)
I will not be _____(bild) for my dinner at this restaurant until I have eaten it.
Will you _____(bild) me a playhouse?

**Brake Break** (brāk)
Don't be so rough! You could _____(brāk) that toy!
A worker on the job will take a _____(brāk) every once in a while to get some rest.
A truck driver will _____(brāk) his truck in order to avoid danger.
It is better to drive with the accelerator than the _____(brāk).

**Colonel Kernel** (k(ə)rn-(ə)l)
Just think of the scrumptious food _____ (k(ə)rn-(ə)l) Sanders can make out of just a _____ (k(ə)rn-(ə)l) of corn!

## Dew Do Due (do͞o)

"How _____ (do͞o) you _____ (do͞o)?" said the _____ (do͞o) to the blades of grass, glistening in the sun. But the grass was not grateful and said, "You're only giving me what is _____ (do͞o) me."

## Feat Feet (fēt)

It was quite a _____ (fēt) for Tom to walk five miles through the blizzard to get help for his grandfather. His _____ (fēt) and hands were pretty cold after walking so far.

## Find Fined (fīnd)

Oh, that driver is going to be mad to _____ (fīnd) out that he has been _____ (fīnd) sixty dollars for parking in the wrong place!

## Hoarse Horse (hō ə rs)

Can a _____(hō ə rs) have a whinny that sounds _____(hō ə rs) if that _____(hō ə rs) isn't feeling well?

## Lie Lye (lī)

When my dad made soap, he would purchase the _____ (lī) that is used in the soap-making process. His mother used to make her own _____ (lī) from wood ashes. I still have my dad's last bar of soap, which has a note that says, "Made with Boraxo."
When he was a boy, his mother threatened to wash his mouth out with soap if he told a _____ (lī). Perhaps it can be said that telling a _____ (lī) can be cured by using _____ (lī), which is made from ashes. Every _____ (lī) should be burned in a fire anyway!
I am not feeling well and need to _____ (lī) down for a while. I will lay my book on the end table before I _____ (lī) down to take a nap.

**Made Maid** (mād)

A Sun _____ (mād) Raisins box shows a picture of a young _____ (mād). Is this _____ (mād) the young woman who _____ (mād) the raisins?

**Morning Mourning** (môr-ning)

Good _____ (môr-ning), Glory! I have brought you a _____ (môr-ning) glory, a flower of great beauty! Do you hear that _____ (môr-ning) dove singing?

If that bird is called a _____ (môr-ning) dove, then why is she singing in the evening instead of the _____ (môr-ning)?

**Pause Paws** (pôz)

Watch that raccoon _____ (pôz), look at you, and then feel for the food with his _____ (pôz), not taking his eyes off you.

**Raise Rays Raze** (rāz)

Are you going to _____ (rāz) corn or soybeans this year?

The _____ (rāz) of the sun will cause the crops to grow well if there is plenty of water.

We need to _____ (rāz) the old barn; it is no longer safe.

**Rain Reign** (rān)

It would be tragic if it did not _____ (rān) for the entire _____ (rān) of a king. How would he collect taxes from the farmers if there was no _____ (rān) to water their crops? All would be discontent, and the king's _____ (rān) would be very frustrating. May it _____ (rān) in season always!

**Road Rode Rowed** (rōd)

I _____ (rōd) past the _____ (rōd) that branched off from this one and then wondered what I missed by not choosing to take that _____ (rōd).

When it started to get dark, we _____ (rōd) our boat to shore.

**Scent Sent Cent ¢** (sent)

I can remember when a gumball cost 1___ (sent).

That skunk _____ (sent) a very repulsive _____ (sent) when he was scared by a mountain lion.

I know a lady named Maxine who could not even smell the _____ (sent) of a skunk! She was the only one who could stand to be in the kitchen at a camp after the skunk sprayed his _____ (sent) there!

Do you suppose that is why people say, "He raised a stink," when someone is mad about not getting his or her own way and complains bitterly and loudly? Such an attitude is not worth one _____ (sent). Maybe if he realized he was acting like a skunk he'd mend his ways!

**Soar Sore** (sō(ə)r)

How can that eagle _____ so high when it has a _____ wing?

**Stair Stare** (sta(ə)r)

Don't _____ (sta(ə)r) at a person who has tripped on a _____ (sta(ə)r). It will embarrass him even more.

# Level 6 Crossword

ACROSS

1  Water falling from the sky
3  The feet of an animal
7  Travel by boat with oars
8  To ride the wind
11 Delivered via the Post Office
12 Construct
14 Earth surrounded by water
16 An untruth
17 Where cars can travel
21 A way to go higher in a house
22 Words sound same, meaning differs
23 Water that condenses on plants
26 To render useless
28 Created
29 A person who helps another
31 Unable to talk properly
32 To give help
33 On the end of my legs
35 Space between rows of chairs
36 Used in making soap
37 Rule of a king

DOWN

1  Beams from the sun
2  The pedal that stops the car
4  A charge for doing wrong
5  A damaged area of the body
6  Accomplish
9  To lift
10 A woman who serves in a hotel
11 A smell, usually pleasant
12 To charge for services
13 Finished a ride
15 An animal featured in a Rodeo
18 A rank in the military
19 The time of day at sunrise
20 Very sad
21 To gawk
24 To level to the ground
25 A very difficult task
27 One seed
30 What is owed
33 To possess what was lost
34 To stop for a while

# Level 6 Word Search

```
C O L O N E L G L E N R E K R Q Z A N K
D N L Y P D T N N Y G R D H A D L I Y L
G D G X N T L I M L A R O F I N E D J P
D J B M R V G N Z Z E A T S N B W B N B
M T M C E Y G R E U R T E P T R R T V E
Q N E R R S X O D S Y T B I A A R A Y T
N N M B W T I M E H O R S E L U I L K Z
T R L D T A B A Q D M N L J P D S R Q E
M L X D K R V I R M A I D A D M N E V N
B U I L D E Q T L K Y R W R O A D E L E
D L T R E R O S E L L S J M T M D Z N M
F E M M T B R Z Y E E G G J V O S O M Y
E K W I A S J O G N F D R N R B H O B Q
A G S I Q T E L W M G J M Z I P R E A Q
T L S J Y R N N K E M I D N O N D E N R
E L L L F S W E T P D N E M K I R P A T
E T V I Y J R Q C L M K O R A M W U R K
R Q N A D B Z M T S P H Z G A D D R O B
O D R W B M V L Z Z X M M D R G N G T M
Z N D N Q X B Z N M D B E N Z D T N Y Z
```

Homophone
Aid
Aide
Aisle
Billed
Build
Brake
Break
Cent
Colonel
Dew
Do
Due
Feat
Feet
Find
Fined
Hoarse
Horse
Isle
Kernel

Lie
Lye
Made
Maid
Morning
Mourning
Pause
Paws
Rain
Raise
Rays
Raze
Reign
Road
Rode
Rowed
Scent
Sent
Soar
Sore
Stair
Stare

# LEVEL 7

Please write (rīt) the correct answers in the spaces provided.

**Air Heir Eyre** (âr)(a(ə)r)
Why does that girl put on an _____ (âr) as if she is better than I?
It must be because she is an _____ (âr) to her father's estate.
In Charlotte Bronte's story of Jane _____ (âr), Jane becomes
an _____ (âr) to her uncle's estate after many years of abuse
at the hands of her Aunt Reed as well as Mr. Brokelhurst at Lowood
School.

**Bait Bate** (bāt)
I had to _____ (bāt) my breath while I waited to see if the bear
would swallow the _____ (bāt).

**Ball Bawl** (b(ô)l)
Don't take that _____ (b(ô)l) away from that baby or he will
_____ (b(ô)l) until he can hardly breathe.

**Born Borne** (bō(ə)rn)
Lilly has _____ (bō(ə)rn) much sorrow since her little child was
_____ (bō(ə)rn) with many birth defects.

**Bough Bow** (bou)
The theater was decorated with a lovely _____ above the
curtain that beautifully set off the dancers taking a _____ after
their performance.

**Caller Collar** (kôl-(ə)r)

The _____ (kôl-(ə)r) on the phone was a lady who could sew very well. She said she could make an nice _____ (kôl-(ə)r) for a man's shirt.

**Cymbal Symbol** (sim-b(ə)l)

A _____ (sim-b(ə)l) in a marching band is a musical instrument that is very loud.

A _____ (sim-b(ə)l) is very quiet because it is an object that represents something intangible like an idea. The American flag is a _____ (sim-b(ə)l) of freedom.

**Die Dye** (dī)

It breaks my heart that so many soldiers must _____ (dī) in battle.

One can even use coffee to _____ (dī) fabric to make a quilt look old.

**Foul Fowl** (fou(ə)l)

Having a bad attitude causes one to be in a _____ (fou(ə)l) mood.

A bad smell is a _____ (fou(ə)l) odor.

A chicken is happy if it is well fed and free from danger. That chicken is a _____ (fou(ə)l) without a _____(fou(ə)l) attitude!

A ball that goes outside the line is a _____(fou(ə)l) ball.

Mischievous behavior is _____(fou(ə)l) play.

Not abiding by the rules in a hockey game is _____(fou(ə)l) play.

Water _____(fou(ə)l) are fun to watch, like geese in a lake.

**Grate Great** (grāt)

I will _____ (grāt) some carrots for a salad.

That sound will _____ (grāt) on my nerves! (Not really. It just made an interesting sentence.)

Please place some wood on the fireplace _____ (grāt).

Abraham Lincoln was a _____ (grāt) president.

**Groan Grown** (grōn)

At the family reunion I know Greg will want to _____ (grōn) when he hears comments from all the little old ladies about how much he has _____ (grōn) since the last reunion!

**Hoes Hose** (hōz)

I use a garden _____(hōz) to water my plants. My husband_____ (hōz) the garden for me to keep weeds away and to let the water from the _____ (hōz) get to the roots of the plants.

After working hard, I take a shower and then put on a pair of _____ (hōz) when I dress up to go somewhere special.

**Knead Need** (nēd)

Mother will _____ (nēd) to _____ (nēd) the bread dough before shaping it into loaves for baking. She will also _____ (nēd) to preheat the oven before baking the raised loaves. Boy, is it ever going to smell good in her kitchen when the bread is baking!

**Liar Lyre** (lī(ə)r)

One must always be truthful or risk having the reputation of a _____ (lī(-ə)r).

A _____ (lī(-ə)r) is a musical instrument the ancient Greeks used to play that is a bit like a harp but was small enough to be held in the musician's arms.

**Moose Mousse** (mo͞os)

A _____ (mo͞os) is an animal with very large antlers. A _____ (mo͞os) certainly does not want to eat _____ (mo͞os), though _____ (mo͞os) makes a nice dessert for people. Then there is a kind of _____ (mo͞os) that a person uses for his or her hair!

**Peer Pier** (pi(ə)r)

It is fun to walk under the _____ (pi(ə)r) at low tide and _____ (pi(ə)r) at the seagulls foraging for their dinner.

**Rapped Rapt Wrapped** (rapt)

The children's faces were the picture of wonder as they beheld with _____ (rapt) attention Mary Poppins rising into the sky with her blue coat _____ (rapt) around her thin body. The children remembered how Mary Poppins _____ (rapt) the floor with her umbrella when she needed to get their attention and then said, "Spit, spot."

**Seam Seem** (sēm)

A _____ (sēm) is made by sewing two pieces of fabric together close to the edge by hand or by sewing machine. Do you know why a seamstress should use a narrower _____ (sēm) to sew a quilt block than when sewing a _____ (sēm) for a dress? It is so there is not so much trimming to do since there are many _____ (sēms) in a quilt block and a quilt block is much smaller than a dress. It may _____ (sēm) like a lot of work to make a quilt block, and it is!

It may _____ (sēm) to you that I am a good seamstress. It is true. Thank you! I use a 5/8" _____ (sēm) for a garment and a ¼" _____ (sēm) for a quilt block.

**Side Sighed** (sīd)

The puppy _____ (sīd) and then rolled over onto its other _____ (sīd) and went back to sleep.

**Sighs Size** (sīz)

Judy _____ (sīz) every time she sees a label that reads, "One _____ (sīz) fits all." To her the label should read, "One _____ (sīz) fits nobody."

**Some Sum** (s(ə)m)

A _____ (s(ə)m) is the total number when two or more numbers are added together. For example, 2 + 2 = 4.

_____ (s(ə)m) is a bit more than a few, which is maybe two or three.

_____ (s(ə)m) students have trouble with a difficult _____ (s(ə)m) but can do easy problems successfully.

**Tide Tied** (tīd)

I put on my shoes and _____ (tīd) them tightly, ready to go home since the _____ (tīd) was coming in and I would no longer be able to walk the beach.

"Time and _____ (tīd) wait for no man." [8]

**Toad Towed** (tōd)

That _____ (tōd) jumped so far I bet he could have _____ (tōd) a log had it been attached to his leg!

**To Too Two 2 Tutu** (to͞o)

My name is Too. I have a friend

Who comes along with me everywhere I go.

His name is O, and he travels along with my o.

Together, our name is spelled t-o-o, _____(to͞o). Our name means "also."

I want to go and he must come _____(to͞o). He wants to come also. Please never forget my friend O, for we need to look "OO" to go anywhere together.

Look! I took my friend _____(to͞o)!

_____(to͞o) can also mean excessive. Eight cookies was _____(to͞o) many to eat at one time! I ate _____(to͞o) much!

A _____(to͞o) with only one o means I will do something. _____(to͞o) do …

_____

8 http://www.brainyquote.com/quotes/quotes/g/geoffreych165940.html

I want _____(to̅o) swim and _____(to̅o) go to the store.

Now there is another to, meaning direction, short for *toward*.

I went _____(to̅o) the kitchen to get an apple.

Then, _____(to̅o) spell the number ____ (to̅o), use the letters *t-w-o*: _____(to̅o)!

So, I want _____(to̅o) go _____(to̅o) the store _____(to̅o) buy a popsicle. My friend wants _____(to̅o) come _____(to̅o), so we will buy _____(to̅o) popsicles.

Then we will go to ballet class, where we each will wear a _____(to̅o to̅o) _____ (to̅o) make us feel like real dancers!

Now, I know I have spent a lot of time on this homophone. The reason I spent so much time on it is that I see the <u>too</u> mistake everywhere! Do you, <u>to</u>? Oops, I mean "_____(to̅o)!"

**Whose Who's** (ho̅oz)

_____ (ho̅oz) afraid of the big, bad wolf?

He _____ (ho̅oz) desire it is to stay away from danger.

**Wood Would** (wŏod)

_____ (wŏod) you please stoke the fire with some dry _____ (wŏod)? I _____ (wŏod) if I could. We need to bring in _____ (wŏod) before the rainstorm because wet _____ (wŏod) is too hard to burn.

**Yoke Yolk** (yōk)

The dictionary says <u>yolk</u> can be pronounced two different ways, either yōk or yōlk. We will choose yōk.[9]

A _____ (yōk) binds two animals together so a more experienced animal can train a young one.

The _____ (yōk) of an egg is the yellow part.

---

[9] *Webster's Encyclopedic Unabridged Dictionary of the English Language* 1989

# Level 7 Crossword

ACROSS

2  2
4  A baby will _____ if unhappy
7  Go in a direction
8  A large frog
10  An animal found in Alaska
12  Numbers added together
14  Right or left part of
15  Jane _____ by Charlotte Bronte
18  A decoration of greenery
19  Pieces of fabric stitched together
20  Gotten taller
22  Loud musical instrument
23  The moon creates from gravity
25  One who inherits
26  The neck of a garment
29  Color white fabric
32  Words sound same, meaning differs
34  Wooden beam holding two oxen together
37  Lifts firewood in a fireplace
38  A person who tells a falsehood
39  Mixing dough or clay
41  Which person
43  Where boats can dock
44  A toy babies like
45  How big or small
46  Put on hook to catch fish
47  To carry
48  Ballerina costume
49  Necessary

DOWN

1  Yellow part of an egg
3  Burn in fireplace
4  To hold in suspense
5  A small amount or number
6  To pull along behind
9  Garden tools
11  Represents an idea
12  A deep breath
13  A very bad odor
14  Appear
16  A way to water a garden
17  Come from mother
21  Encased
22  Visitor
23  To bind together
24  Took and exhaled a deep breath
27  Knocked
28  Asking a favor
29  End of life
30  Oxygen
31  A musical instrument
33  A dessert
35  Bird
36  Also
37  Wonderful
40  Intense concentration
42  Sigh deeply
43  Look very carefully
46  Curtsy

# Level 7 Word Search

```
Y T O O D Z P Q G T Z Y W X R J T J P B K T Y D
B K B N Z Y V W D Y B Y D T R J V Q E K L T P B
D Q L T Z L M B H P M R D L P T R N D E O J T L
W J N R W T H O M O P H O N E C R I S E Y R O R
E L L A B Y B N J R S N Z Q O O E O N K J B L Y
K T B Z L P R N B G E E M L B W H B L O M X Y N
P B A Y Z A T G J W Q L L J Z L M T W Y X W D P
J J P R I V U D T V N A L N T Y N R C Y M B A L
D Y T L G K T J Y B R J Q A T A A R D S O J M Y
E W W V L D U R O D Q M R W C P E A V R I D T H
H M O O S E B W R A P P E D P I E R N N Y G O R
G L J U R W A E R E E P M E P N G W G E W E H Q
I N S D L P I D R B V A D R K H G U O B S N E S
S W N I N D T O J Y E N V R Z T B P Q M A R L M
M O B D D Q N O R S E L L X B R O Q N O Y Y T D
J R I A G E P W Y Q N R N S A S Y A R L P T J M
M G Y Z V X R D R Y K I E P N T Y G D N D K D X
T I D E Q T Q D E D N E T Y M Y Q M L S I Z E K
Y X Y J M G I T P J M H E D Z M Z X B U E L M T
T Y K Y R B A E W K T S E F M U S M L O O M Y M
Q L J N Y B D M D T S W O N Y D B M L B L F O T
T B M N N L Q D U O W E B L X G W J X J V D S
D Y B Y J Z Q N O T L E Z J J R W Y D Q N L Q R
B X N N W W K M D T D K D D B R K J M Q J R G D
```

| | |
|---|---|
| Homophone | Mousse |
| Air | Need |
| Bate | Peer |
| Bait | Pier |
| Ball | Rapped |
| Bawl | Rapt |
| Born | Seam |
| Borne | Seem |
| Bough | Side |
| Bow | Sighed |
| Caller | Sighs |
| Collar | Size |
| Cymbal | Some |
| Die | Sum |
| Dye | Symbol |
| Eyre | Tide |
| Foul | Tied |
| Fowl | To |
| Grate | Too |
| Great | Toad |
| Groan | Towed |
| Grown | Tutu |
| Heir | Two |
| Hoes | Whose |
| Hose | Wood |
| Knead | Would |
| Liar | Wrapped |
| Lyre | Yoke |
| Moose | Yolk |

# LEVEL 8

Please write (rīt) the correct answers in the spaces provided.

**Altar Alter** (ôl-t(ə)r)
Building all those homes will _____ (ôl-t(ə)r) the landscape.
I must _____ (ôl-t(ə)r) my dress in order for it to fit correctly.
Elijah built an _____ (ôl-t(ə)r), poured water on it, and then called upon God to send fire down from heaven.

**Aught Ought** (ôt)
I really _____(ôt) to help someone I see who is in need. It is not for _____ (ôt) that I do it.

**Band Banned** (band)
The marching _____(band) used to march down Main Street until the city council _____(band) all parades from that busy street.

**Boar Bore** (bō(ə)r)
Watch out for that wild _____(bō(ə)r). He will _____ (bō(ə)r) holes in your yard and ruin it.
Why do you keep watching that TV program? It is such a _____(bō(ə)r)!

**Brews Bruise** (bro͞oz)
My father _____(bro͞oz) a fresh pot of coffee every morning.
I ran into the coffee table and caused a huge _____(bro͞oz) on my leg.

40

**Bunion Bunyan** (b(ə)n-y(ə)n)

Poor Paul _____ (b(ə)n-y(ə)n)! He walked so far that his right foot developed a _____ (b(ə)n-y(ə)n) because he couldn't find shoes big enough for his feet!

**Capital Capitol** (kap-(ə)t-(ə)l)

"That's just _____ (kap-(ə)t-(ə)l)!" exclaimed Joe when his eighth grade teacher said they would visit the state _____ (kap-(ə) t-(ə)l) that spring.

**Check Czech** (chek)

The travel agent will _____ (chek) to see if the _____ (chek) Republic is on the list of tours for next summer.

**Coarse Course** (kō(ə)rs)

Of _____ (kō(ə)rs) I would like to wear clothes that are soft and not _____ (kō(ə)rs). It makes it much easier to sit still in that geometry _____ (kō(ə)rs) I am taking.

**Fish Phish** (fish)

What kind of a hook does a computer hacker use to _____ (fish) for information that is private to your computer? Is it anything like the hook used to catch a real _____ (fish) in a lake?

**Flew Flue** (flo͞o)

A bird _____ (flo͞o) into the _____ (flo͞o) and had a smoky, sooty surprise!

**For Fore Four** (fō(ə)r)

The golfer took _____ (fō(ə)r) tries to hit the ball. Then the ball went so wild that he cried, "_____ (fō(ə)r)!" to warn the people on the sidelines, _____ (fō(ə)r) they could get really hurt by a flying golf ball.

**Gnu Knew New** (no͞o)

I _____(no͞o) that a _____(no͞o) is an African antelope, but it was _____(no͞o) knowledge to my friend.

**Grim Grimm** (grim)

The Brothers _____(grim) wrote or recorded fairy tales that really were _____(grim), in my opinion!

**Heed He'd** (hēd)

_____ (hēd) be wise to _____(hēd) the advice of his grandpa.

**Higher Hire** (hī(ə)r)

Will you _____(hī(ə)r) me? I want to climb _____(hī(ə)r) on the corporate ladder, and I will if you _____(hī(ə)r) me for this job.

**Holy Wholly** (hō-lē)

A _____(hō-lē) God wants us to be _____(hō-lē) his.

**Loot Lute** (lo͞ot)

The beautiful _____(lo͞ot), which is like a large guitar with a round back, was part of the _____(lo͞ot) that was stolen from the museum.

**Mary Marry Merry** (mer-ē)

The dictionary has each of these words pronounced a little differently, but I pronounce them ALL as (mer- ē), so:
Sweet _____(mer-ē),
Whom will you _____(mer-ē)?
To whom shall you say, "I do?"
What man will be _____(mer-ē)
When you choose him to _____(mer-ē),
When you promise to him you'll be true?
"_____(mer-ē) Christmas!"

42

**Nay Neigh** (nā)

A _____(nā) is a happy sound from a horse.

_____(nā) is a very old way to say no.

**Oar Or Ore** (ō(ə)r)

"Dip, dip, and swing," let us sing as we paddle a canoe, each holding one _____ (ō(ə)r).

Tom can wail _____ (ō(ə)r) he can sing when he wields the pickax to find _____ (ō(ə)r) in his mine.

**Pair Pare Pear** (pā(ə)r)

The baby's mother will _____(pā(ə)r) the skin off the _____(pā(ə)r) for her baby since the baby has no teeth with which to chew.

Kelly is very young, but she is still very proud of her new _____(pā(ə)r) of shoes.

**Pray Prey** (prā)

We must _____(prā) or else we could fall _____(prā) to all kinds of evil.

**Profit Prophet** (präf-(ə)t)

I will _____(präf-(ə)t) by listening to a true _____(präf-(ə)t).

The store sells goods at a slightly higher price than their purchase price in order to make a _____(präf-(ə)t).

**Real Reel** (rē(ə)l)

I will _____(rē(ə)l) in a fish and dance a _____(rē(ə)l) when I catch it. My cousins own some _____(rē(ə)l) estate on the lake, so I can go fishing often. I share some fish with my grandmother, who always bakes me a cake in thanks for the fish. What a _____(rē(ə)l) reward that is!

**Rote Wrote** (rōt)

Mozart _____(rōt) the song, "Twinkle, Twinkle Little Star" (at least that's what we call it). Many children learn to play that song by _____(rōt) on the piano or violin and read the musical notes much later.

**Sioux Sue** (so͞o)

The _____(so͞o) are a very important American Indian tribe.
My friend _____(so͞o) is a _____(so͞o).
Hopefully _____(so͞o) will never need to _____(so͞o) anyone for doing something illegal against her.

**Stake Steak** (stāk)

The miner will _____(stāk) his claim so that all the minerals he discovers while digging will be his.
Yum! That _____(stāk) smells delicious!
I usually plant bush beans, but next year I want pole beans to climb up a _____(stāk).

**Taught Taut** (tôt)

My dad _____(tôt) me how to keep the fishing line _____(tôt) so my fish wouldn't get away.

**Threw Through** (thro͞o)

Tommy _____(thro͞o) the ball so hard and so high that it went _____(thro͞o) the window!

**Wait Weight** (wāt)

I must _____(wāt) in the hall before seeing the doctor so the nurse can take my blood pressure and find out my _____(wāt).

# Level 8 Crossword

**ACROSS**

3 Memorize mechanically
5 Change
7 Either
8 Channel in a chimney
10 Two of a kind
11 Nothing
14 Ghastly, sinister
15 Pay attention
16 Instruct
18 Pure
20 Paddle for a boat
22 Proper name of storyteller
27 Bound legally as man and wife
28 Class
29 Genuine
31 An African antelope
34 Altogether
37 Mother of Jesus Christ
38 To inspect
40 Deformity of the foot
42 Area of worship
45 Happy sound a horse makes
48 Valuables taken by force
49 Not stopped
52 Past tense of to throw
55 Wood or metal marker or support
56 To take off the skin
57 Seer
58 In front
59 Aware
61 Past tense of to fly
62 Words sound same, meaning differs

**DOWN**

1 Because; to whom it is done
2 A fruit
4 Measure on a scale
6 Moral obligation
7 Metal
9 A trout is a _____
10 Victim
12 Tight
13 Opposite of old
17 Above
19 Indian Tribe
21 Round
23 Happy
24 Group of musicians
25 Cook
26 Folk character
30 A people
32 No
33 Name
35 Gain more
36 Wonderful
39 Rough
40 Blood under the skin
41 My youngest granddaughter is 4
43 To seek illegally on a computer
44 To make a hole
46 Wild pig
47 Meat for food
48 A musical instrument
50 Accepted for work for pay
51 State Legislature meets
53 Past tense of to write
54 Not allowed
56 Talking to God
60 Pause

45

# Level 8 Word Search

```
C H G U O R H T H K G T L T R C W J Q Q Q D K
A E G Y S T Q I A R A E U O Y H M Q R Q P R G
P N S R I T R M I U E E B A O E M M M T N D M
I M B R O E E M P R G R T L T C V E H S I H P
T D O W U T M H K L U H L S B K Z R R H N A Y
O A U E X O E Y P I T Y T S R B E Z C R B Q V
L U G L R P C J S O L T T B E W O E T A Y J Y
E G H F M R Q E L O R A H Z W R Z A N R E A L
T H T P H E E D H L K P E I S C O D R M A R Y
U T E R Y F Q H O E T N M R G W R O T E T L J
L A X O M O Z O S N B D O F A H U N T N W J B
R O Z F T R T N E I G H H I O P E N E M N Y N
C A P I T A L S M W F O R S N R L R G W W W Y
V R A T X N R Y E A M R U U L U E R I A P Q T
Q W N E M A A N N O R Q O E B J B Q R G Q G R
J Y R R O R K A P R W R F B A N N E D R W W G
M O M C P T Y H P E E Q Y L D M P T A Z Q P L
B G I Y B N O P I R Q T F L U E G T K W B Q M
K Q R K U N T G P G E N L J B W L J V L J M B
T Z G B E M H L B W D Y Z A B A K Z N X Y Z X
J N Y J R T Y L Z B B B N N W T R V Y W L B N
```

| | |
|---|---|
| Homophone | Lute |
| Altar | Mary |
| Alter | Marry |
| Aught | Merry |
| Band | Nay |
| Banned | Neigh |
| Boar | New |
| Bore | Oar |
| Brews | Or |
| Bruise | Ore |
| Bunion | Ought |
| Bunyan | Pair |
| Capital | Pare |
| Capitol | Pear |
| Check | Phish |
| Coarse | Pray |
| Course | Prey |
| Czech | Profit |
| Fish | Prophet |
| Flew | Real |
| Flue | Reel |
| For | Rote |
| Fore | Sioux |
| Four | Sue |
| Gnu | Stake |
| Grim | Steak |
| Grimm | Taught |
| Heed | Taut |
| Higher | Threw |
| Hire | Through |
| Holy | Wait |
| Knew | Weight |
| Loot | Wholly |
| | Wrote |

46

# LEVEL 9

Please write (rīt) the correct answers in the spaces provided.

**A choir Acquire** (ə-'kw ī (ə)r)
_____ (ə-'kw ī (ə)r) at the community center is about
to _____(ə-'kw ī (ə)r) a new conductor.

**Ail Ale** (ā(ə)l)
Something will definitely _____ (ā(ə)l) me if I drink that bottle of
_____(ā(ə)l)!

**Allowed Aloud A loud** (ə-loud)
Talking _____(ə-loud) in _____(ə-loud) voice is not
_____(ə-loud) in the library.

**Berth Birth** (b(ə)rth)
The mother horse is soon going to give _____ (b(ə)rth) to her
foal. We must be sure to give a wide enough _____(b(ə)rth)
in her stall to make it as easy as possible for her.

**Cede Seed** (sēd)
I am afraid if our country does not _____ (sēd) to our enemy, we
will be destroyed and our powers taken by force.
The gardener will sow the _____ (sēd) when all danger of frost
has passed.

**Chord Cord** (kō)(ə)rd)
A _____ (kō)(ə)rd) is a kind of a rope, but a _____(kō)(ə)rd)
is not something that can tie one _____ (kō)(ə)rd) to another
since a _____ (kō)(ə)rd) is a musical sound.

**Cite Sight Site** (sīt)

To list my source of information in my paper is to _____(sīt) the source and give another credit for using that author's ideas.

Will you show me the _____(sīt) where the walnut grove is to be planted?

The blossoms on the almond trees are a glorious _____(sīt) in the spring!

**Cruise Cruse Crews** (krōoz)

My husband and I are going on a _____ (krōoz) to Alaska this August. The _____ (krōoz) working on such ships are so helpful!

The pastor took a little _____(krōoz) of oil when he went to the hospital to visit a patient for whom he wanted to pray.

**Dawning Donning** (dôning)

Cheryl is _____(dôning) her new dress for the prom. She looks as lovely as the _____(dôning) of a new day!

**Desert Dessert** (di-z(ə)rt)

It is very, very bad to _____(di-z(ə)rt) someone in the _____(di-z(ə)rt) with no water to drink. However, it is very nice to offer a _____(di-z(ə)rt) of a snow cone on a hot day!

**Faint Feint** (fānt)

The soldier recovered from feeling _____ with fear when he realized there was a _____ planned to protect his unit.

**Genes Jeans** (jēnz)

Gene's _____(jēnz) and Jean's _____(jēnz) look very similar. They will enjoy country line dancing in their new _____(jēnz) and cowboy boots.

Both Jean's _____(jēnz) and Gene's _____(jēnz) transmit heredity.

**Guise Guys** (gīz)

I am not very fond of the phrase, "you _____"; I much prefer the way the people in the South say, "Y'all," instead.

Tom came dressed in all white, under the _____ of being an orderly at the rest home, so he could visit an aging neighbor.

**Hew Hue Hugh** (hyo͞o)

The lumberjacks are able to _____(hyo͞o) many logs very skillfully.

The paint store carries paint cards displaying the _____(hyo͞o) of many different colors.

I know a fine gentleman whose name is _____(hyo͞o).

**In choir Inquire** (in-'kwī(ə)r)

I will _____(in-'kwī(ə)r) whether or not I can be _____ (in-'kwī(ə)r) next season.

**LA La** (lä)

_____ (lä) is the sixth note of diatonic scale in solmization (See DO.)

Shelly sang her own little tune with the nonsense syllable "___(lä), ___(lä), ___(lä), ___(lä)" as she skipped down the sidewalk.

**Laps Lapse** (laps)

There was finally a _____(laps) in Jenni's crying. She was overtired and distraught because her swimming coach made her do so many _____(laps) across the pool.

**Meeting Meting** (mēting)

Sam went to the home association _____(mēting) to learn how to keep his neighborhood a safe place.

The judge is _____(mēting) out justice to those convicted of breaking the law.

**Patience Patients** (pā-shən(t)s)
A nurse must often show great _____ when dealing with her _____ in a hospital.


**Pi Pie** (pī)
A mathematician, after working all day solving equations with _____(pī), will want to go home and eat _____(pī) for dessert. That _____(pī) will certainly increase the circumference of his stomach!


**Pleas Please** (plēz)
We cannot ignore the _____(plēz) of the people trapped inside the burning building.
_____(plēz) call 911 for help!
_____(plēz) listen to the _____(plēz) of anyone, even when his or her cry is not verbal.
Wait here a minute, if you _____(plēz).


**Praise Prays Preys** (prāz)
A wise person _____(prāz) before making an important decision.
The devil _____(prāz) on those who are not protected.
A thankful person will _____(prāz) God in all situations and thus maintain a good attitude.


**Principal Principle** (prin(t)-s(ə)p(ə)l)
A school _____(prin(t)-s(ə)p(ə)l) must be a person of high _____(prin(t)-s(ə)p(ə)l) in order to guide the lives of the teachers and children under his or her care.

**Rest Wrest** (rest)

I can't always _____(rest) and wait for Tommy to let go of a toy. If he's playing with a dangerous knife, I must _____(rest) it from him and explain later!

Good, better, best,

Never let it _____(rest)

Until your good is better

And your better, best![10]

**Rot Wrought** (r(ô)t)

The army _____(r(ô)t) a great victory and brought hope to all the soldiers.

The wooden handle of a tool will _____(r(ô)t) if left outdoors for a very long time, but the blade will just rust.

**Sic Sick** (sik)

Did you know you can make a mistake on purpose and avoid getting a red pen mark on your paper from your teacher? You do it by writing the word (_____) (sik) just after the intentional mistake to say, "I know it is a mistake." Do you think that will work on your next spelling test? (I don't either.) It should work on an essay, though.

Now if you stay up late too many nights in a row studying, you will probably get _____(sik), so don't study too late! It is no fun to be _____(sik).

---

[10] Quote from St. Jerome.

**Sign Sine** (sīn)

Did you understand that? Just know _____(sīn) belongs in mathematics.

Watch for a _____(sīn) that says stop and then turn right at that corner.

A very hot face can be a _____(sīn) that you have a fever.

Would you please _____(sīn) your name to the check you have written?


**Steal Steel** (stē(ə)l)

_____(stē(ə)l) is a metal, an iron that contains carbon.

My favorite bowl is a stainless _____(stē(ə)l) bowl because it won't break and is fairly light.

The passengers knew the plane would crash, so they had to _____(stē(ə)l) themselves against the blow.

Don't leave valuable things in your car in plain sight. Someone may be tempted to _____(stē(ə)l) them.


**Suede Swayed** (swād)

A naughty boy in school dragged three fingers up the _____(swād) jacket of our teacher to show his displeasure at her while we were gathered around her desk. He thought she was a skunk. (I was equally naughty because I didn't like the teacher either, and I giggled about what he did.)

The palm trees _____(swād) in the tropical breeze.

**Suite Sweet** (swēt)

It's nice for a family to rent a _____(swēt) in a hotel so they can all be near each other. Sometimes the housekeeping staff will leave a bit of _____(swēt) candy on the pillow. It would be _____(swēt) of us to leave a tip!

Johann Sebastian Bach wrote more than one _____(swēt) of dances for several different instruments.

**Tear Tier** (ti(ə)r)

A _____(ti(ə)r) is what my eye will shed if I fall down a _____(ti(ə)r).

**Vain Vane** (vān)

In _____(vān), Mr. Connor mounted the weather _____(vān) on the barn, for the barn burned to the ground.

A _____(vān) in our body carries blood back toward the heart.

**Yore You're** (yō(ə)r)

_____(yō(ə)r) wise if you study the times of _____(yō(ə)r) and learn the wise and foolish things that people have done so that _____(yō(ə)r) not inclined to repeat their mistakes.

# Level 9 Crossword

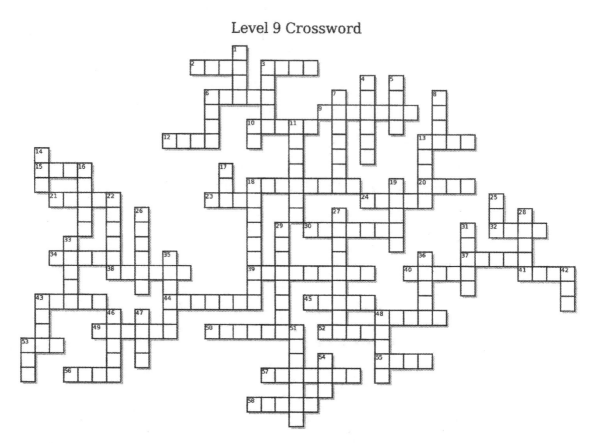

ACROSS

2  Indicates the wind direction
3  Not feeling well
6  Napped Fabric
9  People gathered for purpose
10  Cries for help
12  Fruitless
13  Gardener plants
15  Repetitions in a swimming pool
18  People cared for medically
20  Name
21  Workers
23  Produced when crying
24  Lose consciousness
30  Fashioned
32  Rope
34  Pretending
37  Talking to God
38  Abandon
39  Leading position
40  Casual pants
41  Levels
43  Honey and sugar are _____
44  Ask
45  Spoken to be heard
48  Small container
49  Commend
50  Permitted
52  Space
53  Cut
55  Cease from working when tired
56  Group of people
57  To put on
58  Decoy military maneuver

DOWN

1  Grant by treaty
3  Iron (metal with carbon)
4  Dish out
5  Mathematical function
6  Validate a check
7  Sweets at the end of a meal
8  Long years past
10  Mathematical term
11  Get possession
13  My eyes give it to me
14  Beverage
16  Take what is not owned
17  Dessert with a crust
18  Code of conduct
19  Come from a mother
22  Back and forth
25  Intentional
26  To try to make happy
27  Words sound same, meaning differs
28  Pull forcefully
29  Calm in difficult situation
31  To stop for a moment
33  Grouping
35  Sail, stopping at ports
36  Responsible for hereditary
42  Decay
43  Place
46  Wanting to harm
47  Credit a source
48  Simultaneous musical notes
51  Morning
53  Gradation of color
54  Sick

# Level 9 Word Search

```
T J L B R P L W R E S T G P Y B Y M N T K Q P
N M P J R A Z L L M K R T Y Q M Q E B Y Y R L
I J P E E G T E L P I C N I R P S A L O U D H
E R Y T B N J C E T I U S G G A N B Y J A T J
F S S Y M T L R Y L L A N P E U D Q D D R I B
S W E E T J Z E T B A I L L A V Y E S I G N L
D O N N I N G W L E N P P E K L Y S B E N I S
N T M E D D D S P W A I I N D A M U N I A V C
D H Q C U M E K A J Z R E C W E P R A Y S I B
E G S N G H S D T S E R I S N A W C T R T D L
S I T E G M S X J N L N P N J I C O T E O T X
I S E I D S E D E E S Y T V N L R Q L R Y T L
U B E T N K R E S I U R C N A V K P U L R B D
G T L A T M T J G E N O H P O M O H L I A M V
K J E P E R N R V B K T S J C K V L D S R Y K
L J L T S D E G C E D E L I Q W T H E R P E E
H R I I R R N S P R A I S E R N N N T A O T B
U N C O N I E D E U S J J O I H E Q T R I C M
G K H N T Q X I Q D L J U A M G E I P S E B V
H C Q E N Q U B T Y L G F Z X L E W L Y B B D
T Y E N G T B I P T H M K L T N T P E T O B B
Z M V A P P W P R T B N T Q T P K W A K D R B
N R R V L B Z X L E R Y G S M B D P S Y M R E
```

Homophone
Acquire
Ail
Ale
Allowed
Aloud
Berth
Birth
Cede
Chord
Cite
Cord
Crews
Cruise
Cruse
Dawning
Desert
Dessert
Donning
Faint
Feint
Genes
Guise
Guys
Hew
Hue
Hugh
Inquire
Jeans
Laps
Lapse
Meeting
Meting

Patience
Patients
Pi
Pie
Pleas
Please
Praise
Prays
Preys
Principal
Principle
Rest
Rot
Seed
Sic
Sick
Sight
Sign
Sine
Site
Steal
Steel
Suede
Suite
Swayed
Sweet
Tear
Tier
Vain
Vane
Wrest
Wrought
Yore

# LEVEL 10

Please write (rīt) the correct answers in the spaces provided.

**Bread Bred** (bred)
The cattleman _____(bred) cattle to be strong for their long drive to market. His wife made _____(bred) for the cowboys' journey.

**But Butt** (b(ə)t)
It was not supposed to be able to be done, _____(b(ə)t) Gene chose to _____(b(ə)t) one board against another to make a table big enough for his family.

**Chute Shoot** (sho͞ot)
Tom can _____(sho͞ot) a bow and arrow and also _____(sho͞ot) a basketball into the hoop ten times in a row! When he comes home, Tom must put his basketball uniform into the laundry _____(sho͞ot).

**Core Corps** (kō(ə)r)
I ate the whole apple until just the _____(kō(ə)r) was left.
My grandson wants to be part of the Marine _____(kō(ə)r) when he grows up.

**Crewel Cruel** (kro͞o)-(ə)l)
It would be very _____(kro͞o)-(ə)l) to throw the _____(kro͞o)-(ə)l) embroidery my sister had started into the fire just because I was mad at her for the moment.

56

**Hall Haul** (hôl)

Jerry offered to _____(hôl) the box of trash down the _____(hôl) for the janitor. Then Jerry will load his truck and _____(hôl) the box to the dump.

**Hertz Hurts** (h(ə)rts)

Not telling the truth _____(h(ə)rts) your reputation.

It _____(h(ə)rts) your hands to trim roses if you don't wear garden gloves.

_____(h(ə)rts) are a measure of electricity. It is also the name of a rent-a-car company.

**Idle Idol** (īd-(ə)l)

An _____(īd-(ə)l) neither speaks nor hears. It is useless because it is _____(īd-(ə)l). An _____(īd-(ə)l) only gives false hope and is not worthy of worship.

**Lichen Liken** (lī-k(ə)n)

_____(lī-k(ə)n) will seem to suddenly come to life after a rainstorm, showing up on the bark of trees or on rocks. I _____ (lī-k(ə)n) that sudden burst of life to what happens to me when I eat some food after feeling weak from working too hard and long in the yard. I come back to life!

**Links Lynx** (ling(k)s)

A chain is made of many _____(ling(k)s). They say a chain is only as strong as its weakest link. The _____(ling(k)s) would certainly hope for a weak link in a chain if he happened to be caught in a trap!

**Miner Minor** (mī-n(ə)r)

My widowed grandmother, no matter how poor and needy the family became, would never allow any of her sons to become a _____(mī-n(ə)r). It was just too dangerous, in her opinion.

Particularly her _____(mī-n(ə)r) son was never permitted to become a _____(mī-n(ə)r). He was much too young! Instead, they were encouraged to work in the woods.

**Mustard Mustered** (m(ə)s-t(ə)rd)
My dad used to eat _____(m(ə)s-t(ə)rd) and red lead (ketchup) in the navy and even called those condiments by the naval terms after he was _____(m(ə)s-t(ə)rd) out of the service.
Tommy _____(m(ə)s-t(ə)rd) up the courage to ask the food vendor for some _____(m(ə)s-t(ə)rd) for his hot dog.

**Not Knot Naught** (nôt)
It is _____(nôt) for _____(nôt) that the nun worked at the leper colony. Her caring attention tied a _____(nôt) of love between those whom she served and the one who strengthened her for service.

**Rout Route** (raout)
Those wild boars seem to have a _____(raout) through the farmer's fields to find the best places to _____(raout) out some tasty roots.

**Sear Seer** (si(ə)r)
The _____(si(ə)r) told the wayward man that wicked people will _____(si(ə)r) in eternal punishment.
A good cook will _____(si(ə)r) the meat to hold in the juices and then finish cooking it at a lower temperature.

**Sees Seize Seas** (sēz)
The goal of pirates is to _____(sēz) the valuable treasure on a merchant vessel. When the captain of a merchant ship _____(sēz) a pirate ship, alarm will _____(sēz) him, and he will attempt to sail the high _____(sēz) to escape.

**Sole Soul SOL** (sōl)

The pilot on an airplane wants flight attendants to count each _____(sōl) onboard the aircraft.

The _____(sōl) of a flight attendant's shoe must not be slick or else the shoes might cause him or her to slip.

The flight attendant was the _____(sōl) survivor of the plane crash.

_____(sōl) is the fifth degree of the diatonic scale which can be shortened to SO in order to not say LA afterward by mistake. (See DO.)

**Staid Stayed** (stād)

The attention the soldiers gave their commanding officer was _____(stād).

Have you _____(stād) at the St. George Hotel in Pine Grove, California?

**Straight Strait** (strāt)

A _____(strāt) is a narrow space that connects two bodies of water.

How large of a ship can still make it through the_____(strāt) of Magellan?

You will probably need a ruler to be able to draw a line that is perfectly _____(strāt).

**Tare Tear** (ta(ə)r)

A _____(ta(ə)r) is a weed that I would like to _____(ta(ə)r) out of my garden!

**Thyme Time** (tīm)

Next _____(tīm) I will be sure to include _____(tīm) when I cook that dish.

**Vale Veil** (vā(ə)l)

"The Little Brown Church in the _____(vā(ə)l)" is a hymn about a country church in a valley.[11] At that church, there have been many weddings in which a bride has worn a beautiful _____(vā(ə)l) when marching down the aisle to meet her groom.

**Waist Waste** (wāst)

Haste makes _____(wāst).

Taste makes _____(wāst).

_____(wāst) not, want not.

**Way Weigh** (wā)

I go out of my _____(wā) to _____(wā) all the vegetables I purchase at the market.

---

[11] https://en.wikipedia.org/wiki/The_Little_Brown_Church

# Level 10 Crossword

ACROSS

1  A path to take
2  Stomach area
6  One who digs in the earth for metal
8  Except
10 Valley
13 Inanimate object of worship
14 Very mean
17 To pull apart forcefully
18 Capture by force
20 Painful
23 Nothing
24 Narrow passage in a building
29 Lock in juices of meat
31 Not crooked
34 Rope tied together
38 Squander
39 Understands, visualizes
40 Words sound same, meaning differs
41 Fed on _____ and water
42 The part of a person that lives forever
43 Rental Car Company
44 Connecting units of a chain
45 Not working
46 Remained

DOWN

1  To measure the heaviness
3  A spice
4  Dig with the nose
5  A covering to obscure the face
7  Purposeless
9  Hours, minutes, seconds
11 Center
12 Similar to
15 Narrow body of water
16 Genetics chosen
17 A weed
19 A condiment
21 Take a picture
22 Gathered
25 Wildcat with tufts on the ears
26 Under age
27 Embroidery
28 A plant
29 Predicts events
30 A course of travel
32 Steady
33 Move a load
35 Bodies of fresh water
36 Channel to move objects
37 Group of military men
39 Bottom of one's foot

# Level 10 Word Search

```
T W R N N N T L K T S Q R T X M V S H U R T S K
L R W J B R E A D M Y E P Z L Z E D R J R P D B
R A M X M W I Z T K N N A T J A Z V V Z R M V B
Y M G D T X T D Q R M O W S R S E E S W I Y Y K
L Y G B C R Y P O L B H Z E T Z B Z M N K B K D
L Q B O E X Q T R L Y P X U I K K Q O W Q N Q T
W K R H N Z O L L A H O B E J G R R T V T O N Y
D P T T C O P Z G L S M S Y D P H I B E Z D T P
S D L R H Z L D L Z K O D Q M D M B B I G L D V
M N U S J D Z E B P N H L L Y E D M Y L X P D W
X E O J M W T B W K I D B J S T R A I G H T T K
L S N U J U N C Z E L W A S T E Y O Y B T Y J R
Y O T G G N S W O D R D J N L L N P U H T M T W
D U K A D H B T X R M C S T R A I T Y T R A E T
Z L W M I D T B A N E N E K I L L M H T E M M D
B X N Y L D T Q E R Y T K L Z Y E A S W D M D L
P R Q N J X Q H K V D D H L T E U I S E R R M L
Q N E X Y I C J V L M W R G T L A Y R E T Y L G
V G B D V I D P R T E E J U U W Q E S U E M Q J
G A G D L K N L X T N L H M N A T R O T L R D W
T B L T P T B R E I O C O T T S N R K W A G D P
P N J E Y Y K L M Z W N A S U T P W R X R Y X Q
X L G Y V J T M V Q M R K M Z J U Z Q N J B E J
Y D Z T V Q D J L Q E N J B W M Q B X D B M Y D
```

| | |
|---|---|
| Homophone | Naught |
| Bread | Nought |
| Bred | Rout |
| But | Route |
| Butt | Sear |
| Chute | Seer |
| Core | Seas |
| Corps | Sees |
| Crewel | Seize |
| Cruel | Shoot |
| Hall | Sole |
| Haul | Soul |
| Hertz | Staid |
| Hurts | Stayed |
| Idle | Straight |
| Idol | Strait |
| Knot | Tare |
| Lichen | Tear |
| Liken | Thyme |
| Links | Time |
| Lynx | Vale |
| Miner | Veil |
| Minor | Waist |
| Mustard | Waste |
| Mustered | Way |
| Not | Weigh |

62

# ANSWERS

**A choir Acquire** (ə-'kw ī (ə)r)
<u>A choir</u> at the community center is about to <u>acquire</u> a new conductor.

**Aid Aide** (ād)
A person who will <u>aid</u> another is a special helper called an <u>aide</u>.

**Ail Ale** (ā(ə)l)
Something will definitely <u>ail</u> me if I drink that bottle of <u>ale</u>!

**Air Heir Eyre** (âr)
Why does that girl put on an <u>air</u> as if she is better than I? It must be because she is an <u>heir</u> to her father's estate.
In Charlotte Bronte's story of Jane <u>Eyre</u>, Jane becomes an <u>heir</u> to her uncle's estate after many years of abuse at the hands of her Aunt Reed as well as Mr. Brokelhurst at Lowood School.

**Aisle Isle I'll** (īl)
An <u>aisle</u> is straight, but an <u>isle</u> is round.
<u>I'll</u> help set up the chairs in the auditorium so that an <u>aisle</u> is created for easy access for the patrons.

**Allowed Aloud A loud** (ə-loud)
Talking <u>aloud</u> in <u>a loud</u> voice is not <u>allowed</u> in the library.

**Altar Alter** (ôl-t(ə)r)
Building all those homes will <u>alter</u> the landscape.
I must <u>alter</u> my dress in order for it to fit correctly.
Elijah built an <u>altar</u>, poured water on it, and then called upon God to send fire down from heaven.

**Ate Eight 8 VIII** (āt)

I <u>ate</u> <u>eight</u> cookies and came down with a very bad tummy ache!

Do you know how many eight is? Too many, that's for sure!

I will never eat <u>eight</u> cookies at once again!

The Arabic numeral for the number eight is <u>8</u>.

King Henry <u>VIII</u> started the Church of England.


**Aught Ought** (ôt)

I really <u>ought</u> to help someone I see who is in need. It is not for <u>aught</u> that I do it.


**Aye I Eye** (ī)

<u>Aye-aye</u>, Captain! <u>I</u> can see that ship through the <u>eye</u>glass!


**Bait Bate** (bāt)

I had to <u>bate</u> my breath while I waited to see if the bear would swallow the <u>bait</u>.


**Ball Bawl** (b(ô)l)

Don't take that <u>ball</u> away from that baby or he will <u>bawl</u> until he can hardly breathe.


**Band Banned** (band)

The marching <u>band</u> used to march down Main Street until the city council <u>banned</u> all parades from that busy street.


**Bare Bear** (ba(ə)r)

My favorite toy as a child was a teddy <u>bear</u> that was pink and had polka dots on its tummy.

The <u>bear</u>—not my teddy <u>bear</u>—stripped the tree <u>bare</u> of its bark.

Lydia is my best friend. With her I can <u>bare</u> my soul and tell her my most private secrets.

**Be Bee** (bē)
Pretty buzzing bumble<u>bee</u>,
Won't you please <u>be</u> nice to me?
Please don't sting me!
"To <u>be</u> or not to <u>be</u>,
That is the question."
Do you want to <u>be</u> a <u>bee</u> when you grow up?

**Beat Beet** (bēt)
The recipe says to <u>beat</u> the cake batter for two minutes.
I am going to <u>beat</u> you in a race. I will eat every <u>beet</u> on my plate before you eat all of yours! (That makes Mother mad. It is bad manners to gulp down my food.)

**Beau Bow** (bō)
When I was a little girl, my dad was always the best at tying the <u>bow</u> at the back of my dress. Do you think that a <u>bow</u> at the back of a dress was still in style when I was old enough to have a <u>beau</u>?
The string on a <u>bow</u> must be pulled taut in order to shoot the arrow far enough to reach its target.
One must have a good quality <u>bow</u> to make a cello or violin sound lovely.

**Berth Birth** (b(ə)rth)
The mother horse is soon going to give <u>birth</u> to her foal. We must be sure to give a wide enough <u>berth</u> in her stall to make it as easy as possible for her.

**Billed Build** (bild)
I will not be <u>billed</u> for my dinner at this restaurant until I have eaten it.
Will you <u>build</u> me a playhouse?

**Blew Blue** (blo͞o)
The wind <u>blew</u> away the clouds so now I can see the <u>blue</u> sky.

**Boar Bore** (bō(ə)r)
Watch out for that wild <u>boar</u>. He will <u>bore</u> holes in your yard and ruin it.
Why do you keep watching that TV program? It is such a <u>bore</u>!

**Board Bored** (bō(ə)rd)
When I was bad in school I had to write on the <u>board</u>, "I will behave in school," so many times that I became <u>bored</u>.

**Born Borne** (bō(ə)rn)
Lilly has <u>borne</u> much sorrow since her little child was <u>born</u> with many birth defects.

**Bough Bow** (bou)
The theater was decorated with a beautiful <u>bough</u> above the curtain that beautifully set off the dancers taking a <u>bow</u> after their performance.

**Brake Break** (brāk)
Don't be so rough! You could <u>break</u> that toy!
A worker on the job will take a <u>break</u> every once in a while to get some rest.
A truck driver will <u>brake</u> his truck in order to avoid danger.
It is better to drive with the accelerator than the <u>brake</u>.

**Bread Bred** (bred)
The cattleman <u>bred</u> cattle to be strong for their long drive to market.
His wife made <u>bread</u> for the cowboys' journey.

**Brews Bruise** (bro͞oz)
My father <u>brews</u> a fresh pot of coffee every morning.
I ran into the coffee table and caused a huge <u>bruise</u> on my leg.

**But Butt** (b(ə)t)
It was not supposed to be able to be done, <u>but</u> Gene chose to <u>butt</u> one board against another to make a table big enough for his family.

**Bunion Bunyan** (b(ə)n-y(ə)n)

Poor Paul <u>Bunyan</u>! He walked so far that his foot right developed a <u>bunion</u> because he couldn't find shoes big enough for his feet!

**By Buy Bye** (bī)

I will <u>buy</u> some flowers to give to my friend when I have to say <u>bye</u>.

"<u>Bye</u>" is a quick remark at the end of a phone conversation.

Please pick me some flowers <u>by</u> 2 p.m.

**Caller Collar** (kôl-(ə)r)

The <u>caller</u> on the phone was a lady who could sew very well. She said she could make an nice <u>collar</u> for a man's shirt.

**Capital Capitol** (kap-(ə)t-(ə)l)

"That's just <u>capital</u>!" exclaimed Joe when his eighth grade teacher said they would visit the state <u>capitol</u> that spring.

**Cede Seed** (sēd)

I am afraid if our country does not <u>cede</u> to our enemy, we will be destroyed and our powers taken by force.

The gardener will sow the <u>seed</u> when all danger of frost is has passed.

**Cell Sell** (sel)

If you <u>sell</u> things that are not legal to <u>sell</u> you may end up in a jail <u>cell.</u>

The building block of the human body is the <u>cell.</u>

The phone company tried to <u>sell</u> me a <u>cell</u> phone.

**Check Czech** (chek)

The travel agent will <u>check</u> to see if the <u>Czech</u> Republic is on the list of tours for next summer.

**Chews Choose** (cho͞oz)

Priel <u>chews</u> the stick of gum until there is no taste left in it. She then will have to <u>choose</u> a new piece of gum if she wants it to have a good taste.

**Chord Cord** (kō)(ə)rd)

A <u>cord</u> is a kind of a rope, but a <u>cord</u> is not something that can tie one <u>chord</u> to another since a <u>chord</u> is a musical sound.

**Chute Shoot** (sho͞ot)

Tom can <u>shoot</u> a bow and arrow and also <u>shoot</u> a basketball into the hoop ten times in a row! When he comes home, Tom must put his basketball uniform into the laundry <u>chute</u>.

**Cite Sight Site** (sīt)

To list my source of information in my paper is to <u>cite</u> the source and give another credit for using that author's ideas.
Will you show me the <u>site</u> where the walnut grove is to be planted?
The blossoms on the almond trees are a glorious <u>sight</u> in the spring!

**Coarse Course** (kō(ə)rs)

Of <u>course</u> I would like to wear clothes that are soft and not <u>coarse</u>. It makes it much easier to sit still in that geometry <u>course</u> I am taking.

**Colonel Kernel** (k(ə)rn-(ə)l)

Just think of the scrumptious food <u>Colonel</u> Sanders can make out of just a <u>kernel</u> of corn!

**Core Corps** (kō(ə)r)

I ate the whole apple until just the <u>core</u> was left.
My grandson wants to be part of the Marine <u>Corps</u> when he grows up.

**Creak Creek** (krēk)
The sound of the <u>creek</u> flowing by the house can mask the sound of the <u>creak</u> in the board on the stair when I am trying to sneak back into my room late at night.

**Crewel Cruel** (kro͞o)-(ə)l)
It would be very <u>cruel</u> to throw the <u>crewel</u> embroidery my sister had started into the fire just because I was mad at her for the moment.

**Cruise Cruse Crews** (kro͞oz)
My husband and I are going on a <u>cruise</u> to Alaska this August. The <u>crews</u> working on such ships are so helpful!
The pastor took a little <u>cruse</u> of oil when he went to the hospital to visit a patient for whom he wanted to pray.

**Cymbal Symbol** (sim-b(ə)l)
A <u>cymbal</u> in a marching band is a musical instrument that is very loud.
A <u>symbol</u> is very quiet because it is an object that represents something intangible like an idea. The American flag is a <u>symbol</u> of freedom.

**Days Daze** (dāz)
After so many <u>days</u> of travel on our trip, we were in a <u>daze</u> when we finally arrived at our destination.

**Dawning Donning** (dôning)
Cheryl is <u>donning</u> her new dress for the prom. She looks as lovely as the <u>dawning</u> of a new day!

**Dear Deer** (di(ə)r)
The story of Bambi, the little <u>deer</u>, is <u>dear</u> to my heart.

**Desert Dessert** (di-z(ə)rt)

It is very, very bad to <u>desert</u> someone in the <u>desert</u> with no water to drink. However, it is very nice to offer a <u>dessert</u> of a snow cone on a hot day!

**Dew Do Due** (do͞o)

"How <u>do</u> you <u>do</u>?" said the <u>dew</u> to the blades of grass, glistening in the sun. But the grass was not grateful and said, "You're only giving me what is <u>due</u> me."

**Die Dye** (dī)

It breaks my heart that so many soldiers must <u>die</u> in battle.
One can even use coffee to <u>dye</u> fabric to make a quilt look old.

**DO Doe Dough** (dō)

<u>DO</u> is the first syllable of the diatonic scale in solmization. (The entire scale is <u>DO</u> RE MI FA SOL LA TI <u>DO</u>.)

"<u>DO</u>, a deer, a female deer," are the first few words of the "<u>DO</u>, a Deer" song from the *Sound Of Music.* The female deer is really a <u>doe</u>. My sister used to eat biscuit <u>dough</u> when she was young. *Ugh!* I much preferred oatmeal cookie <u>dough</u>.

**Ewe You** (yo͞o)

Cindy, <u>you</u> were so cute in the Christmas program, playing the <u>ewe</u> resting with her baby lamb near the manger.

**Faint Feint** (fānt)

The soldier recovered from feeling <u>faint</u> with fear when he realized there was a <u>feint</u> planned to protect his unit.

**Fair Fare** (fa (ə)r)

What is the <u>fare</u> to enter the <u>fair</u>?

**Feat Feet** (fēt)
It was quite a <u>feat</u> for Tom to walk five miles through the blizzard to get help for his grandfather. His <u>feet</u> and hands were pretty cold after walking so far.

**Find Fined** (fīnd)
Oh, that driver is going to be mad to <u>find</u> out that he has been <u>fined</u> sixty dollars for parking in the wrong place!

**Fish Phish** (fish)
What kind of a hook does a computer hacker use to <u>phish</u> for information that is private to your computer? Is it anything like the hook used to catch a real <u>fish</u> in a lake?

**Flea Flee** (flē)
That pesky <u>flea</u> had better <u>flee</u> from me!

**Flew Flue** (flo͞o)
A bird <u>flew</u> into the <u>flue</u> and had a smoky, sooty surprise!

**Flour Flower** (flow(ə)r)
When I was young, I used to play with white <u>flour</u> and pretend it was snow.
The crocus is often the first <u>flower</u> to push its way through the snow in the spring.

**For Fore Four** (fō(ə)r)
The golfer took <u>four</u> tries to hit the ball. Then the ball went so wild that he cried, "<u>Fore</u>!" to warn the people on the sidelines, <u>for</u> they could get really hurt by a flying golf ball.

**Foul Fowl** (fou(ə)l)
Having a bad attitude causes one to be in a <u>foul</u> mood.
A bad smell is a <u>foul</u> odor.

A chicken is happy if it is well fed and free from danger. That chicken is a <u>fowl</u> without a <u>foul</u> attitude!
A ball that goes outside the line is a <u>foul</u> ball.
Mischievous behavior is <u>foul</u> play.
Not abiding by the rules in a hockey game is <u>foul</u> play.
Water <u>fowl</u> are fun to watch, like geese in a lake.

**Genes Jeans** (jēnz)
Gene's <u>jeans</u> and Jean's <u>jeans</u> look very similar. They will enjoy country line dancing in their new <u>jeans</u> and cowboy boots.
Both Jean's <u>genes</u> and Gene's <u>genes</u> transmit heredity.

**Gnu Knew New** (no͞o)
I <u>knew</u> that a <u>gnu</u> is an African antelope, but it was <u>new</u> knowledge to my friend.

**Grate Great** (grāt)
I will <u>grate</u> some carrots for a salad.
That sound will <u>grate</u> on my nerves! (Not really. It just made an interesting sentence.)
Please place some wood on the fireplace <u>grate</u>.
Abraham Lincoln was a <u>great</u> president.

**Grease Greece** (grēs)
The smell of bacon <u>grease</u> is a pleasant smell, especially when cooking over a campfire.
Do they cook like that in the nation of <u>Greece</u>?

**Grim Grimm** (grim)
The Brothers <u>Grimm</u> wrote or recorded fairy tales that really were <u>grim</u> in my opinion!

**Groan Grown** (grōn)
At the family reunion I know Greg will want to groan when he hears comments from all the little old ladies about how much he has grown since the last reunion!

**Guise Guys** (gīz)
I am not very fond of the phrase, "you guys"; I much prefer the way the people in the South say, "Y'all," instead.
Tom came dressed in all white, under the guise of being an orderly at the rest home, so he could visit an aging neighbor.

**Hair Hare** (ha(ə)r)
I must be getting healthier. My hair is turning back to gray after having been white for many years! It must be the trace minerals in the blackstrap molasses I have been eating for several months.
A hare is very much like a rabbit.
The hair of a hare is called fur.

**Hall Haul** (hôl)
Jerry offered to haul the box of trash down the hall for the janitor.
Then Jerry will load his truck and haul the box to the dump.

**Heal Heel** (hē(ə)l)
I just bought some shoes that support my feet better. Now perhaps my heel will have a chance to heal so it will no longer be painful when I walk.

**Heard Herd** (h(ə)rd)
The herd of cattle started to stampede when they heard the shot of a rifle.

**Heed He'd** (hēd)
He'd be wise to heed the advice of his grandpa.

**Hertz Hurts** (h(ə)rts)
Not telling the truth <u>hurts</u> your reputation.
It <u>hurts</u> your hands to trim roses if you don't wear garden gloves.
<u>Hertz</u> are a measure of electricity. It is also the name of a rent-a-car company.

**Hew Hue Hugh** (hyo̅o)
The lumberjacks are able to <u>hew</u> many logs very skillfully.
The paint store carries paint cards displaying the <u>hue</u> of many different colors.
I know a fine gentleman whose name is <u>Hugh</u>.

**Higher Hire** (hī(ə)r)
Will you <u>hire</u> me? I want to climb <u>higher</u> on the corporate ladder, and I will if you <u>hire</u> me for this job.

**Him Hymn** (him)
A favorite <u>hymn</u> of many people is "In the Garden."
God loves to hear a <u>hymn</u> of praise sung to honor <u>him</u>.

**Hoarse Horse** (ho̅ərs)
Can a <u>horse</u> have a whinny that sounds <u>hoarse</u> if that <u>horse</u> isn't feeling well?

**Hoes Hose** (ho̅z)
I use a garden <u>hose</u> to water my plants. My husband <u>hoes</u> the garden for me to keep weeds away and to let the water from the <u>hose</u> get to the roots of the plants. After working hard, I take a shower and then put on a pair of <u>hose</u> when I dress up to go somewhere special.

**Hole Whole** (ho̅l)
If I have a <u>hole</u> in my purse, my <u>whole</u> collection of coins could be lost.

**Holy Wholly** (hō-lē)
A <u>holy</u> God wants us to be <u>wholly</u> his.

**Hour Our** ((ou)(ə)r)
The soup kitchen has asked us to spend just one <u>hour</u> of <u>our</u> time serving food to the homeless so the needy people can have a chance to eat.

**Idle Idol** (īd-(ə)l)
An <u>idol</u> neither speaks nor hears. It is useless because it is <u>idle</u>. An <u>idol</u> only gives false hope and is not worthy of worship.

**In Inn** (in)
I was disappointed when my husband told me there was no vacancy <u>in </u>the <u>inn</u> for us to stay.

**In choir Inquire** (in-'kwī(ə)r)
I will <u>inquire</u> whether or not I can be <u>in choir</u> next season.

**Knead Need** (nēd)
Mother will <u>need</u> to <u>knead</u> the bread dough before shaping it into loaves for baking. She will also <u>need</u> to preheat the oven before baking the raised loaves. Boy, is it ever going to smell good in her kitchen when the bread is baking!

**Knew New** (no͞o)
Tina ran outside in the rain in her <u>new</u> shoes even though she <u>knew</u> better. Tina's brother <u>knew</u> their mother would be angry!

**Knows Nose** (nōz)
Priel <u>knows</u> that her <u>nose</u> helps her smell.
She <u>knows</u> sometimes the smell is pleasant and sometimes her <u>nose</u> tells her something *stinks!*

**LA La** (lä)

<u>LA</u> is the sixth note of diatonic scale in solmization. (See DO.)
Shelly sang her own little tune with the nonsense syllable, "<u>La</u>, <u>la</u>, <u>la</u>, <u>la</u>," as she skipped down the sidewalk.

**Laps Lapse** (laps)

There was finally a <u>lapse</u> in Jenni's crying. She was overtired and distraught because her swimming coach made her do so many <u>laps</u> across the pool.

**Liar Lyre** (lī(-ə)r)

One must always be truthful or risk having the reputation of a <u>liar</u>.
A <u>lyre</u> is a musical instrument the ancient Greeks used to play that is a bit like a harp but was small enough to be held in the musician's arms.

**Lie Lye** (lī)

When my dad made soap, he would purchase the <u>lye</u> that is used in the soap-making process. His mother used to make her own <u>lye</u> from wood ashes. I still have my dad's last bar of soap, which has a note that says, "Made with Boraxo."
When he was a boy, his mother threatened to wash his mouth out with soap if he told a <u>lie</u>. Perhaps it can be said that telling a <u>lie</u> can be cured by using <u>lye</u>, which is made from ashes. Every <u>lie</u> should be burned in a fire anyway!
I am not feeling well and need to <u>lie</u> down for a while. I will lay my book on the end table before I <u>lie</u> down to take a nap.

**Lichen Liken** (lī-k(ə)n)

<u>Lichen</u> will seem to suddenly come to life after a rainstorm, showing up on the bark of trees or on rocks. I <u>liken</u> that sudden burst of life to what happens to me when I eat some food after feeling weak from working too hard and long in the yard. I come back to life!

**Links Lynx** (ling(k)s)
A chain is made of many <u>links</u>. They say a chain is only as strong as its weakest link. The <u>lynx</u> would certainly hope for a weak link in a chain if he happened to be caught in a trap!

**Lo Low** (lō)
And <u>lo</u>! The angel of the Lord appeared.
The animals <u>low</u> in the stable, giving thanks for the savior in their own special way.

**Loot Lute** (lo͞ot)
The beautiful <u>lute</u>, which is like a large guitar with a round back, was part of the <u>loot</u> that was stolen from the museum.

**Mail Male** (mā(ə)l)
A little boy is a <u>male</u> who will grow up to be a daddy. Maybe he will work for the post office and deliver <u>mail</u> for a living.

**Main Mane** (mān)
Simba thought he would be the <u>main</u> event when he was big enough to have a <u>mane</u> and a roar!

**Mary Merry Marry** (mer- ē)
Sweet <u>Mary</u>,
Whom will you <u>marry</u>?
To whom shall you say, "I do?"
What man will be <u>merry</u>
When you choose him to <u>marry</u>,
When you promise to him you'll be true?

"<u>Merry</u> Christmas!"

**Made Maid** (mād)
A Sun <u>Maid</u> Raisins Box shows a picture of young <u>maid</u>. Is this <u>maid</u> the young woman who <u>made</u> the raisins?

**Me MI** (mē)
<u>MI</u> is the third tone of the diatonic scale. (See DO)
<u>MI</u> is a name I call myself, according to the "DO, a Deer" song.
Will you sing for <u>me</u>?

**Meat Meet** (mēt)
I would like to <u>meet</u> somebody who prefers <u>meat</u> to tofu for dinner!

**Meeting Meting** (mēting)
Sam went to the home association <u>meeting</u> to learn how to keep his neighborhood a safe place.
The judge is <u>meting</u> out justice to those convicted of breaking the law.

**Might Mite** (mīt)
I <u>might</u> get very annoyed by a <u>mite</u> if it chooses to bite me!

**Miner Minor** (mī-n(ə)r)
My widowed grandmother, no matter how poor and needy the family became, never allowed any of her sons to become a <u>miner</u>. It was just too dangerous, in her opinion. Particularly her <u>minor</u> son was never permitted to become a <u>miner.</u> He was much too young! Instead, they were encouraged to work in the woods.

**Moose Mousse** (mo͞os)
A <u>moose</u> is an animal with very large antlers. A <u>moose</u> certainly does not want to eat <u>mousse</u>, though <u>mousse</u> makes a nice dessert for people. Then there is a kind of <u>mousse</u> that a person uses for his or her hair!

**Morning Mourning** (môr-ning)

"Good <u>morning</u>, Glory! I have brought you a <u>morning</u> glory! Do you hear that <u>mourning</u> dove singing?"

If that bird is called a <u>mourning</u> dove, then why is she singing in the evening instead of the <u>morning</u>?

**Mustard Mustered** (m(ə)s-t(ə)rd)

My dad used to eat <u>mustard</u> and red lead (ketchup) in the navy and even called those condiments by the naval terms after he was <u>mustered</u> out of the service.

Tommy <u>mustered</u> up the courage to ask the food vendor for some <u>mustard</u> for his hot dog.

**Nay Neigh** (nā)

A <u>neigh</u> is a happy sound from a horse.

<u>Nay</u> is a very old way to say, "No."

**Night Knight** (nīt)

The medieval <u>knight</u> was a warrior who wanted to be seen. He had no desire to fight at <u>night</u> when it was dark.

**None Nun** (n(ə)n)

There were <u>none</u> who would volunteer to work at the leper colony except one <u>nun</u> who was willing to risk her life to help the needy. There were <u>none</u> so brave as she! <u>None</u> dare try to talk the <u>nun</u> out of her devotion!

**Not Knot Naught** (nôt)

It is <u>not</u> for <u>naught</u> (<u>nought</u> is also correct) that the nun worked at the leper colony. Her caring attention tied a <u>knot</u> of love between those whom she served and the one who strengthened her for service.

**One Won** (w(ə)n)

Kristy is the <u>one</u> who <u>won</u> the Princess Race at Disneyland.

**Oar Or Ore** (ō(ə)r)

"Dip, dip, and swing," let us sing as we paddle a canoe, each holding one <u>oar</u>.

Tom can wail <u>or</u> he can sing when he wields the pickax to find <u>ore</u> in his mine.

**Pail Pale** (pā(ə)l)

Jack and Jill went up the hill to fetch a <u>pail</u> of water. Jill became <u>pale</u> when Jack fell down and spilled his <u>pail</u> of water!

**Pair Pare Pear** (pā(ə)r)

The baby's mother will <u>pare</u> the skin off the <u>pear</u> for her baby since the baby has no teeth with which to chew.

Kelly is very young, but she is still very proud of her new <u>pair</u> of shoes.

**Passed Past** (past)

In the <u>past</u>, Cheryl always studied and <u>passed</u> all her exams easily, so why is she nervous now?

**Patience Patients** (pā-shən(t)s)

A nurse must often show great <u>patience</u> when dealing with her <u>patients</u> in a hospital.

**Pause Paws** (pôz)

Watch that raccoon <u>pause</u>, look at you, and then feel for the food with his <u>paws</u>, not taking his eyes off you.

**Peace Piece** (pēs)

What <u>peace</u> I have, floating on this lake in my boat. Wouldn't everyone like to have a <u>piece</u> of my happiness?

**Peak Peek** (pēk)

That mountain <u>peak</u> is beautiful in the sunset.

At Christmastime, every child will <u>peek</u> at the presents under the tree!

**Peer Pier** (pi(ə)r)
It is fun to walk under the <u>pier</u> at low tide and <u>peer</u> at the seagulls foraging for their dinner.

**Pi Pie** (pī)
A mathematician, after working all day solving equations with <u>pi</u>, will want to go home and eat <u>pie</u> for dessert. That <u>pie</u> will certainly increase the circumference of his stomach!

**Plain Plane** (plān)
In the United States, the middle of the country is one vast <u>plain</u>.
A carpenter uses a <u>plane</u> to make a wood surface level and smooth.
We go to an airport to catch an airplane but we call it a <u>plane.</u>
It is <u>plain</u> to see that an airstrip is easier to create on the <u>plain</u> than in the mountains. A <u>plane</u> can only land on a <u>plane</u> surface.

**Pleas Please** (plēz)
We cannot ignore the <u>pleas</u> of the people trapped inside the burning building. <u>Please</u> call 911 for help!
<u>Please</u> listen to the <u>pleas</u> of anyone, even when his or her cry is not verbal.
Wait here a minute, if you <u>please</u>.

**Pray Prey** (prā)
We must <u>pray</u> or else we could fall <u>prey</u> to all kinds of evil.

**Prays Preys Praise** (prāz)
A wise person <u>prays</u> before making an important decision.
The devil <u>preys</u> on those who are not protected.
A thankful person will <u>praise</u> God in all situations and thus maintain a good attitude.

**Principal Principle** (prin(t)-s(ə)p(ə)l)
A school <u>principal</u> must be a person of high <u>principle</u> in order to guide the lives of the teachers and children under his or her care.

**Profit Prophet** (präf-(ə)t)
I will <u>profit</u> by listening to a true <u>prophet</u>.
The store sells goods at a slightly higher price than their purchase price in order to make a <u>profit</u>.

**Rain Reign** (rān)
It would be tragic if it did not <u>rain</u> for the entire <u>reign</u> of a king. How would he collect taxes from the farmers if there was no <u>rain</u> to water their crops? All would be discontent, and the king's <u>reign</u> would be very frustrating. May it <u>rain</u> in season always!

**Raise Rays Raze** (rāz)
Are you going to <u>raise</u> corn or soybeans this year?
The <u>rays</u> of the sun will cause the crops to grow well if there is plenty of water.
We need to <u>raze</u> the old barn; it is no longer safe.

**Rapped Rapt Wrapped** (rapt)
The children's faces were the picture of wonder as they beheld with <u>rapt</u> attention Mary Poppins rising into the sky with her blue coat <u>wrapped</u> around her thin body. The children remembered how Mary Poppins <u>rapped</u> the floor with her umbrella when she needed to get their attention and then said, "Spit, spot."

**Ray RE** (Rā)
<u>RE</u> is the second tone of the diatonic scale. (See DO.)
It is beautiful to be in a forest and trace a <u>ray</u> of sunshine as it travels through the tree limbs to the path below.
The <u>ray</u> belongs to an order of fish that has a flat body and eyes on its top side. When snorkeling, it is hard to see the <u>ray</u> as it rests on

the sandy ocean bottom, especially when only occasionally is there a <u>ray</u> of sunshine that reaches the ocean floor. I wonder if the <u>ray</u> can sing, "<u>RE</u>"?

**Read Red** (red)
I <u>read</u> the story of Little <u>Red</u> Riding Hood and liked it very much until I <u>read</u> about the wolf trying to trick the girl and put her in danger.

**Read Reed** (rēd)
Please <u>read</u> me the story of a little girl getting lost in the <u>reed</u> swamp.

**Real Reel** (rē(-ə)l)
I will <u>reel</u> in a fish and dance a <u>reel</u> when I catch it. My cousins own some <u>real</u> estate on the lake, so I can go fishing often. I share some fish with my grandmother, who always bakes me a cake in thanks for the fish. What a <u>real</u> reward that is!

**Rest Wrest** (rest)
I can't always <u>rest</u> and wait for Tommy to let go of a toy. If he's playing with a dangerous knife, I must <u>wrest</u> it from him and explain later!

Good, better, best,
Never let it <u>rest</u>
Until your good is better
And your better, best!

**Right Write Rite Wright** (rīt)
Most people know the difference between <u>right</u> and wrong.
Did you know that a <u>wright</u> is a workman of wood?
With which hand do you <u>write</u>? The left or the <u>right</u>?
We must always strive to do the <u>right</u> thing. A religious <u>rite</u> can help us focus on God in worship so we can ask him to help us do the <u>right</u> thing in every situation.

**Road Rode Rowed** (rōd)

I <u>rode</u> past the <u>road</u> that branched off from this one and then wondered what I missed by not choosing to take that <u>road</u>.

When it started to get dark, we <u>rowed</u> our boat to shore.

**Role Roll** (rōl)

In a family, hopefully there is one member who plays the <u>role</u> of peacemaker.

Gretchen danced the <u>role</u> of Giselle in the ballet, *Giselle.*

At Christmastime it is fun to <u>roll</u> out cookie dough and use a cookie cutter to make a gingerbread man.

At the restaurant we like to ask for a <u>roll</u> instead of the cheese bread they usually offer.

Priel and Natania will <u>roll</u> down the hill at the park, giggling all the time.

**Rose Rows** (rōz)

At the park there were <u>rows</u> and <u>rows</u> of <u>rose</u> bushes of every imaginable color a <u>rose</u> could be.

Shakespeare wrote, "A <u>rose</u> by any other name would smell as sweet," but I think a <u>rose</u> called a stink bud would *not* smell so pretty.

**Rot Wrought** (r(ô)t)

The army <u>wrought</u> a great victory and brought hope to all the soldiers.

The wooden handle of a tool will <u>rot</u> if left outdoors for a very long time, but the blade will just rust.

**Rote Wrote** (rōt)

Mozart <u>wrote</u> the song, "Twinkle, Twinkle Little Star," (at least that's what we call it). Many children learn to play that song by <u>rote</u> on the piano or violin and read the musical notes much later.

**Route Rout** (raout)
Those wild boars seem to have a <u>route</u> through the farmer's fields to find the best places to <u>rout</u> out some tasty roots.

**Sail Sale** (sā(ə)l)
I made a <u>sail</u> out of fabric I purchased on <u>sale</u> at the fabric store. My boat should <u>sail</u> far with such a <u>sail</u>! Maybe I can purchase some boat paint on <u>sale</u> too at the paint store.

**Scene Seen** (sēn)
I have never <u>seen</u> such a beautiful <u>scene</u> in all my life!

**Scent Sent Cent ¢** (sent)
I can remember when a gumball cost 1¢.
That skunk <u>sent</u> a very repulsive <u>scent</u> when he was scared by a mountain lion.
I know a lady named Maxine who could not even smell the <u>scent</u> of a skunk! She was the only one who could stand to be in the kitchen at a camp after the skunk sprayed his <u>scent</u> there!
Do you suppose that is why people say, "He raised a stink," when someone is mad about not getting his or her own way and complains bitterly and loudly? Such an attitude is not worth one <u>cent</u>. Maybe if he realized he was acting like a skunk he'd mend his ways!

**Sea See** (sē)
I want to <u>see</u> the ocean and <u>see</u> for myself the majesty of the waves of the <u>sea</u> crashing on the shore.

**Seam Seem** (sēm)
A <u>seam</u> is made by sewing two pieces of fabric together close to the edge by hand or by sewing machine. Do you know why a seamstress should use a narrower <u>seam</u> to sew a quilt block than when sewing a <u>seam</u> for a dress? It is so there is not so much trimming to do since there are many <u>seams</u> in a quilt block and a quilt block is much

smaller than a dress. It may <u>seem</u> like a lot of work to make a quilt block, and it is!

It may <u>seem</u> to you that I am a good seamstress. It is true. Thank you! I use a 5/8" <u>seam</u> for a garment and a ¼" <u>seam</u> for a quilt block.

## Sear Seer (si(ə)r)

The <u>seer</u> told the wayward man that wicked people will <u>sear</u> in eternal punishment.

A good cook will <u>sear</u> the meat to hold in the juices and then finish cooking it at a lower temperature.

## Sees Seas Seize (sēz)

The goal of pirates is to <u>seize</u> the valuable treasure on a merchant vessel. When the captain of a merchant ship <u>sees</u> a pirate ship, alarm will <u>seize</u> him, and he will attempt to sail the high <u>seas</u> to escape.

## Sew So SO Sow (sō)

<u>SO</u> is the sixth degree of the diatonic scale. (See DO.)

I am <u>so</u> weary after making a quilt for a great-grandson but was <u>so</u> energized by the gratitude of my granddaughter. I will <u>sew</u> again soon!

We think to <u>sow</u> seed by hand is rather old-fashioned, but I still like to spread lawn fertilizer that way.

## Shirley Surely (shû(r)-lē)

<u>Surely</u> you have heard of <u>Shirley</u> Temple, the cute dimpled film star who cheered audiences during the Depression.

## Shoe Shoo (sho͞o)

<u>Shoo</u>, fly, don't bother me
For I belong to somebody!
I must <u>shoo</u> away that fly because I certainly will never be able to get him with my <u>shoe</u>.

**Sic Sick** (sik)

Did you know you can make a mistake on purpose and avoid getting a red pen mark on your paper from your teacher? You do it by writing the word (sic) just after the intentional mistake to say, "I know it is a mistake." Do you think that will work on your next spelling test? (I don't either.) It should work on an essay, though.

Now if you stay up late too many nights in a row studying, you will probably get sick, so don't study too late! It is no fun to be sick.

**Side Sighed** (sīd)

The puppy sighed and then rolled over onto its other side and went back to sleep.

**Sighs Size** (sīz)

Judy sighs every time she sees a label that reads, "One size fits all." To her the label should read, "One size fits nobody."

**Sign Sine** (sīn)

Did you understand that? Just know sine belongs in mathematics.

Watch for a sign that says stop and then turn right at that corner.

A very hot face can be a sign that you have a fever.

Would you please sign your name to the check you have written?

**Sioux Sue** (so͞o)

The Sioux are a very important American Indian tribe.

My friend Sue is a Sioux.

Hopefully Sue will never need to sue anyone for doing something illegal against her.

**Soar Sore** (sō(ə)r)

How can that eagle soar so high when it has a sore wing?

**Sole Soul SOL** (sōl)

The pilot on an airplane wants flight attendants to count each <u>soul</u> onboard the aircraft.

The <u>sole</u> of a flight attendant's shoe must not be slick or else the shoes might cause him or her to slip.

The flight attendant was the <u>sole</u> survivor of the plane crash.

<u>SOL</u>) is the fifth degree of the diatonic scale which can be shortened to SO in order to not say LA afterward by mistake. (See DO.)

**Some Sum** (s(ə)m)

A <u>sum</u> is the total number when two or more numbers are put together. For example, 2 + 2 = 4.

<u>Some</u> is a bit more than a few, which is maybe two or three.

<u>Some</u> students have trouble with a difficult <u>sum</u> but can do easy problems successfully.

**Son Sun** (s(ə)n)

If my <u>son</u> spends a lot of time in the <u>sun</u>, he will get a <u>sun</u>burn.

**Staid Stayed** (stād)

The attention the soldiers gave their commanding officer was <u>staid</u>.

Have you <u>stayed</u> at the St. George Hotel in Pine Grove, California?

**Stake Steak** (stāk)

The miner will <u>stake</u> his claim so that all the minerals he discovers while digging will be his.

Yum! That <u>steak</u> smells delicious!

I usually plant bush beans, but next year I want pole beans to climb up a <u>stake</u>.

**Stair Stare** (sta(ə)r)

Don't <u>stare</u> at a person who has tripped on a <u>stair</u>. It will embarrass him even more.

**Steal Steel** (stē(ə)l)

Steel is a metal, an iron that contains carbon.

My favorite bowl is a stainless steel bowl because it won't break and is fairly light.

The passengers knew the plane would crash, so they had to steel themselves against the blow.

Don't leave valuable things in your car in plain sight. Someone may be tempted to steal them.

**Straight Strait** (strāt)

A strait is a narrow space that connects two bodies of water.

How large of a ship can still make it through the Strait of Magellan?

You will probably need a ruler to be able to draw a line that is perfectly straight.

**Suede Swayed** (swād)

A naughty boy in school dragged three fingers up the suede jacket of our teacher to show his displeasure at her while we were gathered around her desk. He thought she was a skunk. (I was equally naughty because I didn't like the teacher either, and I giggled about what he did.)

The palm trees swayed in the tropical breeze.

**Suite Sweet** (swēt)

It's nice for a family to rent a suite in a hotel so they can all be near each other. Sometimes the housekeeping staff will leave a bit of sweet candy on the pillow. It would be sweet of us to leave a tip!

Johann Sebastian Bach wrote more than one suite of dances for several different instruments.

**Tail Tale** (tā(ə)l)

An elephant has a funny tail,

A fox, a bush one.

But Paul Bunyan could spin a tall <u>tale</u>.
In fact, he *became* one!

**Tare Tear** (ta(ə)r)
A <u>tare</u> is a weed that I would like to <u>tear</u> out of my garden!

**Taught Taut** (tôt)
My dad <u>taught</u> me how to keep the fishing line <u>taut</u> so my fish wouldn't get away.

**Tea Tee TI** (tē)
<u>TI</u> is the seventh note of diatonic scale, sometimes called si. (See DO.)
I like a nice cup of hot <u>tea</u> when I am cold.
Place your golf ball very carefully on the <u>tee</u> so you can start your game with confidence!
When writing a story, sometimes an author will have a character laugh by saying, "<u>tee</u>-hee!"

**Tear Tier** (ti(ə)r)
A <u>tear</u> is what my eye will shed if I fall down a <u>tier</u>.

**Their There They're** (thər)
I thought it was here that I left my book, but I see it over <u>there</u> by the clock. Did you notice that the word *here* is contained in the word *<u>there</u>*? That is a good memory tip: here and <u>there</u> are both places, one close and one far.
The sports fans had <u>their</u> eyes on the star player. <u>They're</u> hoping he will save the game!
<u>They're</u> means "they are." An apostrophe is in place of the letter *a* to make a contraction.
<u>They're</u> afraid of <u>their</u> own shadow over <u>there</u> on that dark street.

**Threw Through** (thro͞o)
Tommy <u>threw</u> the ball so hard and so high that it went <u>through</u> the window!

**Thyme Time** (tīm)
Next <u>time</u> I will be sure to include <u>thyme</u> when I cook that dish.

**Tide Tied** (tīd)
I put on my shoes and <u>tied</u> them tightly, ready to go home since the <u>tide</u> was coming in and I would no longer be able to walk the beach. "Time and <u>Tide</u> wait for no man."

**To Too Two 2 Tutu** (to͞o)
My name is Too. I have a friend
Who comes along with me everywhere I go.
His name is O and he travels along with my *o*.
Together, our name is spelled *t-o-o*, <u>Too</u>. Our name means "also."
I want to go and he must come <u>too</u>. He wants to come also. Please never forget my friend O, for we need to look "OO" to go anywhere together.
Look! I took my friend <u>too</u>!
    <u>Too</u> can also mean excessive. Eight cookies was <u>too</u> many to eat at one time! I ate <u>too</u> much!
A <u>to</u> with only one *o* means I will do something. <u>To</u> do …
I want <u>to</u> swim and <u>to</u> go <u>to</u> the store.
Now there is another <u>to</u>, meaning direction, short for *toward*.
I went <u>to</u> the kitchen to get an apple.
Then, <u>to</u> spell the number <u>2,</u> use the letters *t-w-o*: <u>two</u>!
So, I want <u>to</u> go <u>to</u> the store <u>to</u> buy a popsicle. My friend wants <u>to</u> come <u>too</u>, so we will buy <u>two</u> popsicles.
Then we will go to ballet class, where we each will wear a <u>tutu</u> <u>to</u> make us feel like real dancers!

Now, I know I have spent a lot of time on this homophone. The reason I spend so much time on it is that I see the too mistake everywhere! Do you, to? Oops, I mean <u>too</u>!"

**Toad Towed** (tōd)
That <u>toad</u> jumped so far I bet he could have <u>towed</u> a log had it been attached to his leg!

**Toe Tow** (tō)
It would be a very silly thing to see a tugboat <u>tow</u> my <u>toe</u>! But maybe I can imagine that a tugboat will <u>tow</u> my <u>toe</u> when I don't want to get out of bed in the morning.

**Vain Vane** (vān)
In <u>vain</u> Mr. Connor mounted the weather <u>vane</u> on the barn, for the barn burned to the ground.
A <u>vein</u> in our body carries blood back toward the heart.

**Vale Veil** (vā(ə)l)
"The Little Brown Church in the <u>Vale</u>" is a hymn about a country church in a valley. At that church, there have been many weddings in which a bride has worn a beautiful <u>veil</u> when marching down the aisle to meet her groom.

**Waist Waste** (wāst)
Haste makes <u>waste</u>.
Taste makes <u>waist</u>.
<u>Waste</u> not, want not.

**Wait Weight** (wāt)
I must <u>wait</u> in the hall before seeing the doctor so the nurse can take my blood pressure and find out my <u>weight</u>.

**Way Weigh** (wā)

I go out of my <u>way</u> to <u>weigh</u> all the vegetables I purchase at the market.

**Weak Week** (wēk)

I have had the flu and have felt <u>weak</u> all <u>week</u>.

**Whose Who's** (hōoz)

<u>Who's</u> afraid of the big, bad wolf?
He <u>whose</u> desire it is to stay away from danger.

**Wood Would** (wŏod)

<u>Would</u> you please stoke the fire with some dry <u>wood</u>? I <u>would</u> if I could. We need to bring in <u>wood</u> before the rainstorm because wet <u>wood</u> is too hard to burn.

**Yoke Yolk** (Yōk)

A <u>yoke</u> binds two animals together so a more experienced animal can train a young one.
The <u>yolk</u> of an egg is the yellow part.

**Yore You're** (yō(ə)r)

<u>You're</u> wise if you study the times of <u>yore</u> and learn the wise and foolish things people have done so that <u>you're</u> not inclined to repeat their mistakes.

# Level 1 Crossword

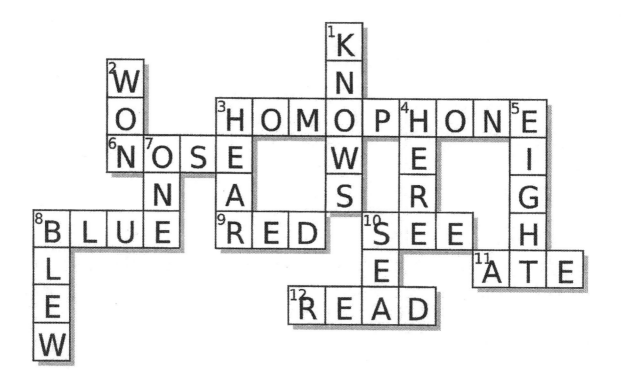

# Level 1 Word Search

H O M O P H O N E
W E L B T S E A G
O B U H S W O N K
N A G L R E D R G
E I T A B E E B D
E S E E R A E O R
E H O E D E N T R
S M H N D E B R T

# Level 2 Crossword

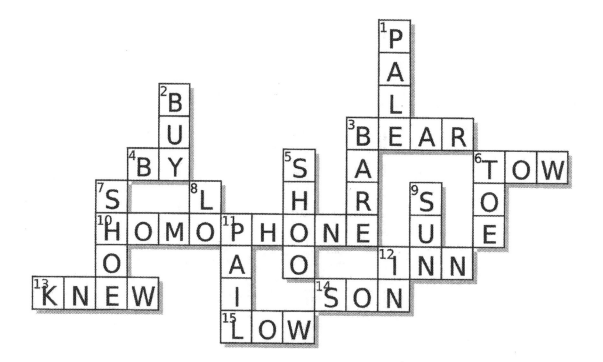

# Level 2 Word Search

H Q L M N N Y N P Y M D P
O D T Y T G W Q A I N A E
M X M T Y E N Q I Y L O M
O N P D N J R J L E H Y N
P L N K Q A N L W S W O L
H T T I E M Y E T O S L O
O E K B S M L O W N T Z T
N D R Y B H E N W R W Y L
E B D A B U O D R S B N T
K Y G N B Q Y O U N D Q N
N E Y K R B J N Q N D Y G
W B V G N B M Z V R T J P

97

# Level 3 Crossword

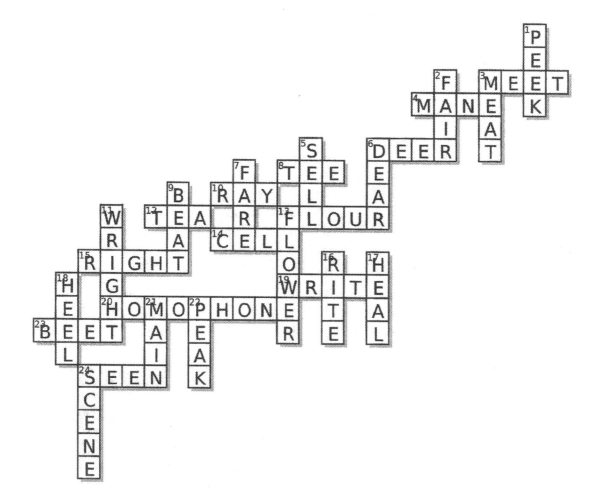

# Level 3 Word Search

# Level 4 Crossword

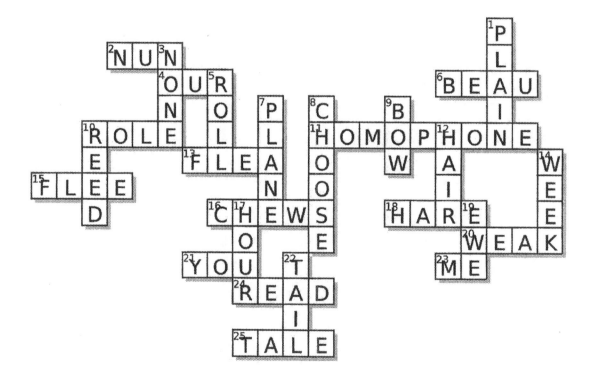

# Level 4 Word Search

# Level 5 Crossword

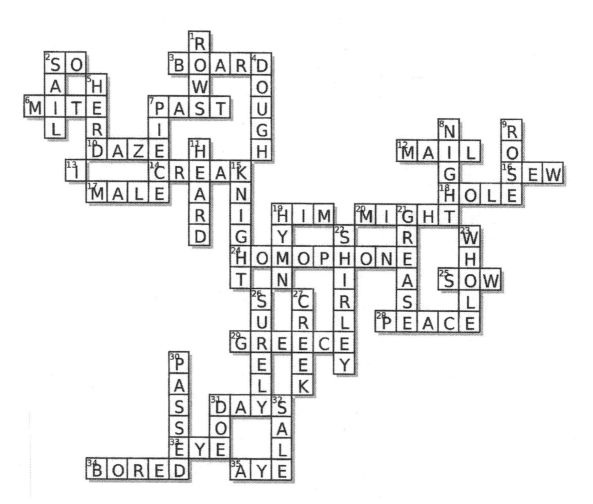

# Level 5 Word Search

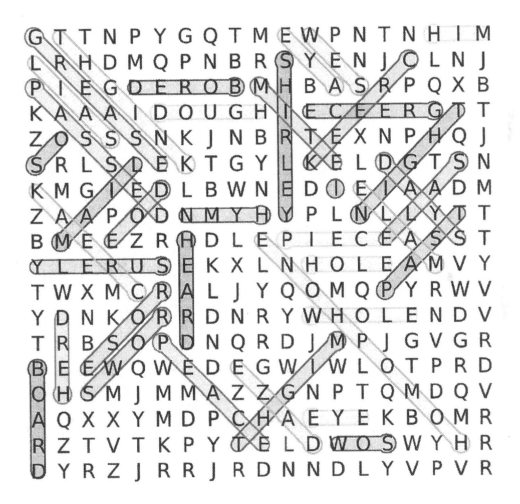

# Level 6 Crossword

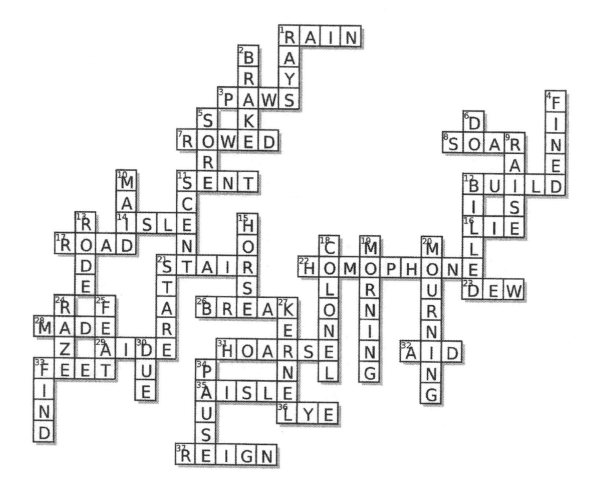

# Level 6 Word Search

```
C O L O N E L G L E N R E K R Q Z A N K
D N L Y P D T N N Y G R D H A D L I Y L
G D G X N T L I M L A R O F I I N E J P
D J B M R V G N Z Z B A T S N B W B N B
M T M C E Y G R E U R T E P T R R T V E
Q N E R R S X O D S Y T B I A A R A Y T
N N M B W T I M E H O R S E L U I L K Z
T R L D T A B A Q D M N L J P D S R Q E
M L X D K R V I R M A I D A D M N B V N
B U I L D E Q T L K Y R W R O A D E L E
D L T R E R O S E L L S J M T M D Z N M
F E M M T B R Z Y E E G G J V O S O M Y
E K W I A S J O G N F D R N R B H O B Q
A G S I Q T E L W M G J M Z I P R E A Q
T L S J Y R N N K E M I D N O N D E N R
E L L L F S W E T P D N E M K I R P A T
E T V I Y J R Q C L M K O R A M W U R K
R Q N A D B Z M T S P H Z G A D D R O B
O D R W B M V L Z Z X M M D R G N G T M
Z N D N Q X B Z N M D B E N Z D T N Y Z
```

105

Level 7 Crossword

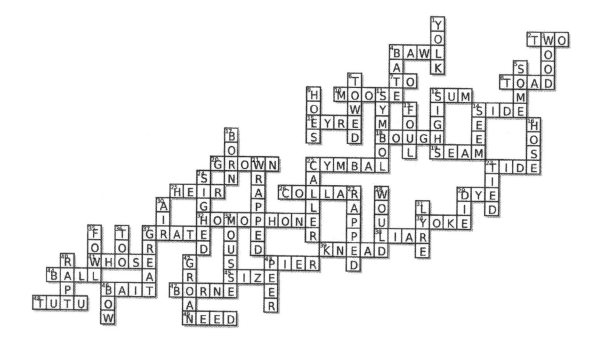

# Level 7 Word Search

```
Y T O O D Z P Q G T Z Y W X R J T J P B K T Y D
B K B N Z Y V W D Y B Y D T R J V O F K L T P B
D Q L T Z D M B H P M R D L P T R N D O J T L
W J N R W T H O M O P H O N E O R I S E Y R O R
E L A B Y B N J R S N Z Q O O E O N K J B L Y
K T B Z L P R N B G E E M L B W H B L O M X Y N
P B A Y Z A T G J W Q L L J Z L M T W Y X W D P
J J P R I V U D T V N A L N T Y N R C Y M B A L
D Y T L G K T J Y B R J Q A T A A R D S O J M Y
E W W V L D U R O D Q M R W C P E A V R I D T H
H M O O S E B W R A P P E D P I E R N N Y G O R
G L J U R W A E R E E P M E P N G W G E W E H Q
I N S D L P I D R B V A D R K H G U O B S N E S
S W N I N D U O J Y E N V R Z T B P Q M A R L M
M O B D D Q N O R S E L L X B R O Q N O Y Y T D
J R I A G E P W Y Q N R N S A S Y A R L P T J M
M G Y Z V X R D R Y K I E P N T Y G D N D K D X
T I D E Q T Q D E D N E T Y M Y Q M L S I Z E K
Y X Y J M G I T P J M H E D Z M Z X B U E L M T
T Y K Y R B A E W K T S E F M U S M L O O M Y M
Q L J N Y B D M D T S W O N Y D B M L B L F O T
T B M N N N L Q D U O W E B L X G W J X J V D S
D Y B Y J Z Q N O T L E Z J R W Y D Q N L Q R
B X N N W W K M D T D K D D B R K J M Q J R G D
```

# Level 8 Crossword

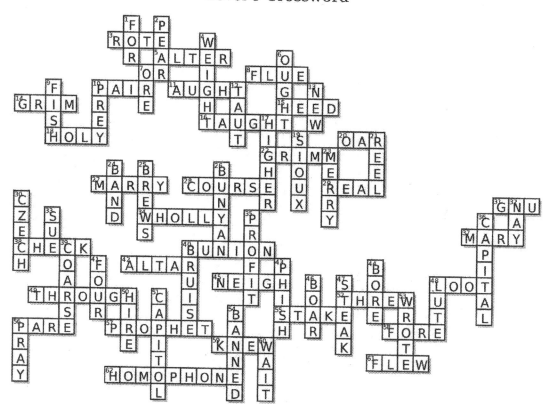

# Level 8 Word Search

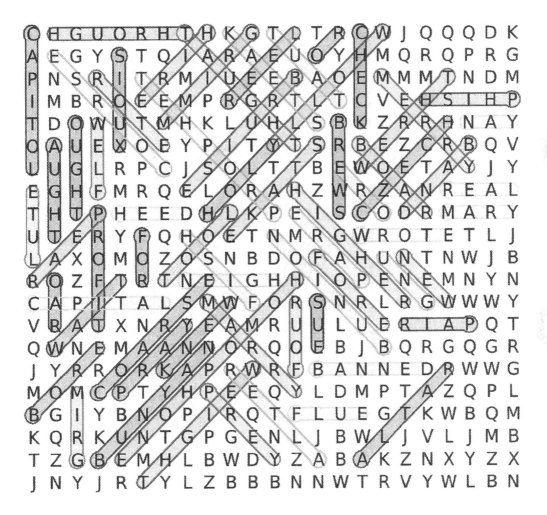

109

# Level 9 Crossword

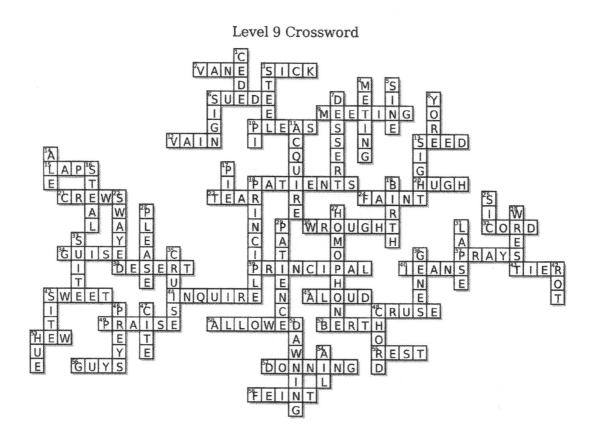

# Level 9 Word Search

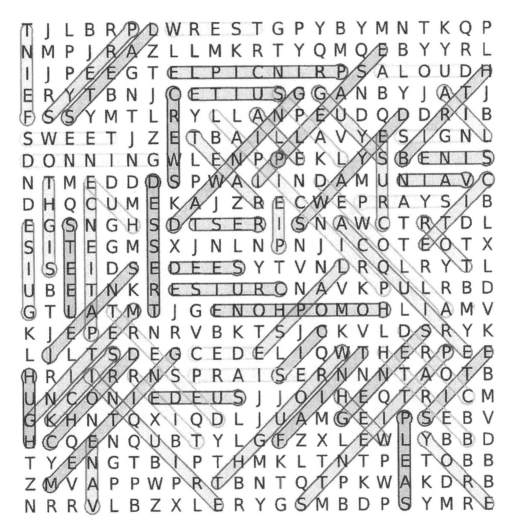

# Level 10 Crossword

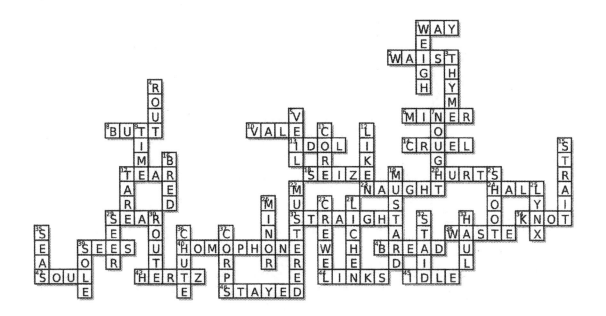

# Level 10 Word Search

```
T W R N N N T L K T S Q R T X M V S H U R T S K
L R W J B R E A D M Y E P Z L Z E D R J R P D B
R A M X M W I Z T K N N A T J A Z V V Z R M V B
Y M G D T X T D Q R M O W S B S E S W I Y Y K
L Y G B O R Y P O L B H Z E T Z B Z M N K B K D
L Q B O E X Q T R D Y P X U K K Q O W Q N Q T
W K R H N Z O L A H O B E J G R R T V I O N Y
D P T T C O P Z G L S M S Y D P H I B E Z D T P
S D L R H Z L D L Z K O D Q M D M B B I G L D V
M N U S J D Z E B P N H L L Y E D M Y U X P D W
X E O J M W T B W K I D B J S T R A I G H T T K
L S N U J U N C Z E L W A S T E Y O Y B T Y J R
Y O T G G N S W O D R D J N L L N P U H T M T W
D U K A D H B T X R M C S T R A I T Y T R A E I
Z U W M I D T B A N E N E K I L M H T B M M D
B X N Y D T Q E R Y T K L Z Y E A S W D M D L
P R Q N J X Q H K V D D H L T B U I S E R R M L
Q N E X Y I C J V L M W R G T L A Y R E T Y L G
V G B D V I D P R T E E J U U W Q E S U E M Q J
G A G D L K N L X T N L H M N A T R O T L R D W
T B L T P T B R E I O C O T T S N R K W A G D P
P N J B Y Y K L M Z W N A S U T P W R X R Y X Q
X L G Y V J T M V Q M R K M Z J U Z Q N J B E J
Y D Z T V Q D J L Q E N J B W M Q B X D B M Y D
```

113

# INDEX

| | | | |
|---|---|---|---|
| Course | Level 8 | Flower | Level 3 |
| Creak | Level 5 | Foul | Level 7 |
| Creek | Level 5 | Flue | Level 8 |
| Crewel | Level 10 | For | Level 8 |
| Cruel | Level 10 | Fore | Level 8 |
| Cruise | Level 9 | Four | Level 8 |
| Cruse | Level 9 | Fowl | Level 7 |
| Crews | Level 9 | Genes | Level 9 |
| Cymbal | Level 7 | Gnu | Level 8 |
| Czech | Level 8 | Grate | Level 7 |
| Dawning | Level 9 | Grease | Level 5 |
| Days | Level 5 | Great | Level 7 |
| Daze | Level 5 | Greece | Level 5 |
| Dear | Level 3 | Grim | Level 8 |
| Deer | Level 3 | Grimm | Level 8 |
| Desert | Level 9 | Groan | Level 7 |
| Dessert | Level 9 | Grown | Level 7 |
| Dew | Level 6 | Guise | Level 9 |
| Die | Level 7 | Guys | Level 9 |
| DO | Level 5 | Hall | Level 10 |
| Do | Level 6 | Hair | Level 4 |
| Doe | Level 5 | Hare | Level 4 |
| Donning | Level 9 | Haul | Level 10 |
| Dough | Level 5 | Heal | Level 3 |
| Due | Level 6 | Heard | Level 5 |
| Dye | Level 7 | Heed | Level 8 |
| Eight | Level 1 | Hertz | Level 10 |
| Ewe | Level 4 | Hew | Level 9 |
| Eye | Level 5 | He'd | Level 8 |
| Eyre | Level 7 | Heel | Level 3 |
| FA | Level 9 | Heir | Level 7 |
| Faint | Level 9 | Herd | Level 5 |
| Fair | Level 3 | Higher | Level 8 |
| Fare | Level 3 | Him | Level 5 |
| Feat | Level 6 | Hire | Level 8 |
| Feet | Level 6 | Hoarse | Level 6 |
| Feint | Level 9 | Hoes | Level 7 |
| Find | Level 6 | Hole | Level 5 |
| Fined | Level 6 | Holy | Level 8 |
| Fish | Level 8 | Horse | Level 6 |
| Flea | Level 4 | Hose | Level 7 |
| Flee | Level 4 | Hour | Level 4 |
| Flew | Level 8 | Hue | Level 9 |
| Flour | Level 3 | | |

| | | | |
|---|---|---|---|
| Hugh | Level 9 | Meat | Level 3 |
| Hurts | Level 10 | Meet | Level 3 |
| Hymn | Level 5 | Merry | Level 8 |
| I | Level 5 | Meting | Level 9 |
| Idle | Level 10 | Meeting | Level 9 |
| Idol | Level 10 | MI | Level 4 |
| I'll | Level 6 | Might | Level 5 |
| In Choir | Level 9 | Miner | Level 10 |
| Inquire | Level 9 | Minor | Level 10 |
| Isle | Level 6 | Mite | Level 5 |
| Jeans | Level 9 | Moose | Level 7 |
| Kernel | Level 6 | Morning | Level 6 |
| Knead | Level 7 | Mourning | Level 6 |
| Knew | Level 2 | Mousse | Level 7 |
| Knew | Level 8 | Mustard | Level 10 |
| Knight | Level 5 | Mustered | Level 10 |
| Knot | Level 10 | Naught | Level 10 |
| Knows | Level 1 | Nay | Level 8 |
| La | Level 9 | Need | Level 7 |
| LA | Level 9 | Neigh | Level 8 |
| Laps | Level 9 | New | Level 2 |
| Lapse | Level 9 | New | Level 8 |
| Liar | Level 7 | Night | Level 5 |
| Lichen | Level 10 | None | Level 4 |
| Lie | Level 6 | Nose | Level 1 |
| Liken | Level 10 | Not | Level 10 |
| Links | Level 10 | Nought | Level 10 |
| Lo | Level 2 | Nun | Level 4 |
| Loot | Level 8 | Oar | Level 8 |
| Low | Level 2 | One | Level 1 |
| Lute | Level 8 | Or | Level 8 |
| Lye | Level 6 | Ore | Level 8 |
| Lynx | Level 10 | Ought | Level 8 |
| Lyre | Level 7 | Our | Level 4 |
| Made | Level 6 | Pail | Level 2 |
| Maid | Level 6 | Pair | Level 8 |
| Mail | Level 5 | Pale | Level 2 |
| Main | Level 3 | Pare | Level 8 |
| Male | Level 5 | Passed | Level 5 |
| Mane | Level 3 | Past | Level 5 |
| Mary | Level 8 | Patience | Level 9 |
| Marry | Level 8 | Patients | Level 9 |
| Me | Level 4 | Pause | Level 6 |
| | | Paws | Level 6 |

| | | | |
|---|---|---|---|
| Peace | Level 5 | Roll | Level 4 |
| Peak | Level 3 | Rose | Level 5 |
| Pear | Level 8 | Rot | Level 9 |
| Peek | Level 3 | Rote | Level 8 |
| Peer | Level 7 | Rout | Level 10 |
| Phish | Level 8 | Route | Level 10 |
| Pi | Level 9 | Rowed | Level 6 |
| Pie | Level 9 | Rows | Level 5 |
| Piece | Level 5 | Sail | Level 5 |
| Pier | Level 7 | Sale | Level 5 |
| Plain | Level 4 | Scene | Level 3 |
| Plane | Level 4 | Scent | Level 6 |
| Pleas | Level 9 | Sea | Level 1 |
| Please | Level 9 | Seam | Level 7 |
| Praise | Level 9 | Sear | Level 10 |
| Pray | Level 8 | Seas | Level 10 |
| Prays | Level 9 | See | Level 1 |
| Prey | Level 8 | Seed | Level 9 |
| Preys | Level 9 | Seem | Level 7 |
| Principal | Level 9 | Seen | Level 3 |
| Principle | Level 9 | Seer | Level 10 |
| Profit | Level 8 | Sees | Level 10 |
| Prophet | Level 8 | Seize | Level 10 |
| Raise | Level 6 | Sell | Level 3 |
| Rapped | Level 7 | Sent | Level 6 |
| Rapt | Level 7 | Sew | Level 5 |
| Ray | Level 3 | Shirley | Level 5 |
| Rays | Level 6 | Shoe | Level 2 |
| Raze | Level 6 | Shoo | Level 2 |
| Rain | Level 6 | Shoot | Level 10 |
| RE | Level 3 | Sic | Level 9 |
| Real | Level 8 | Sick | Level 9 |
| Reel | Level 8 | Side | Level 7 |
| Reign | Level 6 | Sighed | Level 7 |
| Read | Level 1 | Sighs | Level 7 |
| Read | Level 4 | Sight | Level 9 |
| Reed | Level 4 | Sign | Level 9 |
| Red | Level 1 | Sine | Level 9 |
| Rest | Level 9 | Sioux | Level 8 |
| Right | Level 3 | Site | Level 9 |
| Rite | Level 3 | Size | Level 7 |
| Road | Level 6 | So | Level 5 |
| Rode | Level 6 | SO | Level 5 |
| Role | Level 4 | Soar | Level 6 |

| | | | |
|---|---|---|---|
| SOL | Level 10 | Tier | Level 9 |
| Sole | Level 10 | Time | Level 10 |
| Some | Level 7 | To | Level 7 |
| Son | Level 2 | Toad | Level 7 |
| Sore | Level 6 | Toe | Level 2 |
| Soul | Level 10 | Too | Level 7 |
| Sow | Level 5 | Tow | Level 2 |
| Staid | Level 10 | Towed | Level 7 |
| Stair | Level 6 | Two | Level 7 |
| Stake | Level 8 | Tutu | Level 7 |
| Stare | Level 6 | Vain | Level 9 |
| Stayed | Level 10 | Vale | Level 10 |
| Steak | Level 8 | Vane | Level 9 |
| Steal | Level 9 | Veil | Level 10 |
| Steel | Level 9 | Waist | Level 10 |
| Straight | Level 10 | Wait | Level 8 |
| Strait | Level 10 | Way | Level 10 |
| Sue | Level 8 | Weak | Level 4 |
| Suede | Level 9 | Week | Level 4 |
| Suite | Level 9 | Weigh | Level 10 |
| Sum | Level 7 | Weight | Level 8 |
| Sun | Level 2 | Whole | Level 5 |
| Surely | Level 5 | Wholly | Level 8 |
| Sweet | Level 9 | Who's | Level 7 |
| Swayed | Level 9 | Whose | Level 7 |
| Symbol | Level 7 | Won | Level 1 |
| Tail | Level 4 | Wood | Level 7 |
| Tale | Level 4 | Would | Level 7 |
| Tare | Level 10 | Wrapped | Level 7 |
| Taught | Level 8 | Wrest | Level 9 |
| Taut | Level 8 | Wright | Level 3 |
| Tea | Level 3 | Write | Level 1 |
| Tear | Level 9 | Write | Level 3 |
| Tear | Level 10 | Wrote | Level 8 |
| Tee | Level 3 | Wrought | Level 9 |
| Their | Level 5 | Yoke | Level 7 |
| There | Level 5 | Yolk | Level 7 |
| They're | Level 5 | Yore | Level 9 |
| Threw | Level 8 | You | Level 4 |
| Through | Level 8 | You're | Level 9 |
| Thyme | Level 10 | | |
| TI | Level 3 | | |
| Tide | Level 7 | | |
| Tied | Level 7 | | |

Printed in the United States
By Bookmasters